KT-153-081

SEX & SENSIBILITY

Also by Julie Burchill

Love It or Shove It
Damaged Gods
Girls On Film
Ambition

SEX &
SENSIBILITY

· · · · · · · · · ·

Julie Burchill

Grafton
An Imprint of HarperCollins*Publishers*

Grafton
An Imprint of HarperCollins*Publishers*,
77–85 Fulham Palace Road,
Hammersmith, London W6 8JB

A Grafton Original 1992
9 8 7 6 5 4 3 2 1

Copyright © Julie Burchill 1992
'Sex Zombies' Copyright © *Cosmopolitan* 1988

The Author asserts the moral right to
be identified as the author of this work

A catalogue record for this book is
available from the British Library

ISBN 0 00 637858 7

Set in Palacio by Avocet Typesetters, Bicester, Oxon

Printed in Great Britain by
HarperCollinsManufacturing Glasgow

All rights reserved. No part of this publication may be
reproduced, stored in a retrieval system, or transmitted,
in any form or by any means, electronic, mechanical,
photocopying, recording or otherwise, without the prior
permission of the publishers.

This book is sold subject to the condition that it shall not,
by way of trade or otherwise, be lent, re-sold, hired out
or otherwise circulated without the publisher's prior
consent in any form of binding or cover other than that
in which it is published and without a similar condition
including this condition being imposed on the subsequent
purchaser.

Written between 1984 and 1992, these pieces come from
The Face, Arena, Elle, Woman's Journal, the *Mail on Sunday*,
the *Guardian*, the *Tatler*, the *Modern Review*, *20/20* and
Cosmopolitan. A full list of sources is given on p. 265.

ACKNOWLEDGEMENTS

· · · · · · · ·

The author would like to thank Cosmo Landesman for some, but by no means all, of the best lines. And for their helpfulness and generosity, Val Hudson, Maggie Alderson, Jenny Cowley, Sheryl Garratt, Christie Hickman, Dylan Jones, Frances Landesman, Paul and Yvette Levett, Jane Proctor, Cyrus Tadiwala, Jocelyn Targett, Toby Young, Peter York and, most of all, the world's greatest living editor, Mr Stewart Steven.

For Maria

CONTENTS

. . . .

Contents

INTRODUCTION
ARE WRITERS REAL PEOPLE?

. . . .

If a thing's worth doing, it's worth writing about. So why is it that the things which one most likes to do – drink, have sex, be married – are the hardest things to write about well? And perhaps the hardest thing to write about without coming across as a complete and utter div is writing itself.

To write about writing is one tough task. You tiptoe across the page, Tippex at the ready, knowing that one wrong word, one careless cliché, and you'll read like a dweeb. Every paragraph is a potential minefield of preciousness and pomposity. And in between the lines, the word WANKER! winks on and off like neon.

There *must* be a way to do it without subscribing to either the Pansy (writing as pressing wild flowers) or Pugilist (writing as six rounds with Joe Louis) schools of pen-pushing. But how?

Whenever I read writers on writing, I'm proud to call myself a hack. The vices of journalism are plain to see and endlessly itemized, but its virtues – self-deprecation, graft, lack of phoney baloney – are rarely mentioned. Yet it is true that while it's easy to call oneself a journalist or to write about journalism without once sounding like a berk, it's impossible even to *say* the word 'literature' without *(a)* lisping and *(b)* coming over like a Luvvy.

To actors, all the world's a prime-time slot on *Wogan* wherein ideally they will tell you how their trade is one long, loony walk on the wacky side. Sit them down on the squidgy sofa and right on cue they'll whip you up a nice little variation on 'It's A Crazy Profession – We're All A Little Mad!' Literature too suffers from the Luvvy Tendency. Writers love nothing more than to dress up and play exciting roles: pansy, pugilist, priest, shaman, madman, moral guardian, monster of depravity – take your pick. Of course, you don't *have* to be a psychotic/ invert/dypsomaniac/drug fiend to write, but – like the sad little signs in the insurance offices say – it helps!

And just as in every thesp there is a motheaten anecdote about being legless and starkers with Ollie and Peter at three in the morning on some RAF base in Samarkand, so literature has its own Luvvy folklore: from Scott and Zelda going down Broadway on top of a taxi, not waving but drowning, to Papa Hemingway O.D.ing on bullshots, bullfighting and bullshit.

Literary Luvvies, as I have said, tend to come from either the Pansy or Pugilist tradition. But the Pansies are in retreat these days, sent packing by the dirty realists like Richard Ford and Raymond Carver, who actually made a pact that if one of them 'went fag', the other would shoot him, like a dog, and put him out of his misery. With such trigger-happy typists among us, it is perhaps a mercy that great Pansies like Noël Coward (did all his writing in a silk dressing-gown) and Truman Capote (did all his writing prone on a chaise longue) have passed on to the great reading room in the sky. Only the poet Jeremy Reed – who anoints himself with scent and lipstick and slips into something a little more comfortable, like a monk's cowl, before giving the old Remington a right seeing to – is brave enough to toss the gauntlet of effeminacy at the feet of visible virility.

What *is* the Pugilist Pen-Pushers' problem? you may ask. It's easy enough to understand; they are painfully aware that, to most people, and strictly within a historical context, like, squatting in a centrally-heated room making things up all day is not what you'd usually classify as a Proper Job For A Man. This unarticulated critique leads to all sorts of over-compensatory Luvvy theatrics – from actually attempting to spar with professional boxers (US) to a sort of sheepish, roll-your-own, louche lager-swilling laddishness which cannot pass a video arcade without giving Sonic the Hedgehog a good kicking (us).

It is the Pugilist Pen-Pushers who demonstrate better than any other writer how otherwise sane people can take leave of their senses when attempting to justify sedentary, scribbling lifestyle choices. 'If I didn't have writing, I'd be running down the street hurling grenades into people's faces,' says Paul Fussell. ('Of *course* you wouldn't, silly!' you want to shout, while shaking him by the shoulders (in a *caring* sort of way, natch) – you'd just be a sulky old professor, hurling nothing deadlier than bitter sarcastic barbs at your brighter students.) For James Jones writing was 'a desire for self-exposure' *and* 'masochistic', for Thomas Sanchez 'a horseback ride into heaven and hell and back', for Norman Mailer 'agony'. Phew! Did you ever see so many men weep tears of pure testosterone? Tough guys don't dance – they type.

If most male actors dream of playing Hamlet, then most male writers dream of playing Hemingway. It was the papa of them all who changed writing for ever from being something that indoorsy Parisian faggots with trust funds and servants did furtively between asthma attacks in the dead of night to being a bloodsport. It was Hemingway, seeking to define his own tortured masculinity – and to defy his own tiny manhood ('He lacks the serene self-confidence that he is a full-sized man'; Max Eastman) – who portrayed writing as something between a life sentence on the Parchman Farm chain gang and castrating a buffalo with your bare teeth – look Ma, no dental dam!

So it was Hemingway we have to blame for the Pugilist Pen-Pusher wet dream that the writer is a dark force of Nature – Conan the Librarian – a creature of compulsion – driven, unbalanced, possessed! – whose life is one long game of Russian roulette revenge on the whole damn ball-breaking modern world, where men are mice and women have ideological armpits; rather than the white-collar long-luncher with health insurance, a StepMaster and le petit mort(gage) that he nearly always was. But Hem had his Greek Chorus, and they too must shoulder some of the blame: Mailer, Jones, Nelson Algren, Charles Bukowski, Seth Morgan and Ishmael 'Writing Is Fighting' Reed.

Traditionally, Eng. Lit. provided a safe haven for the Pansy Pen-Pushers, usually under the sub-division of Fop or Dandy. From Wilde to Waugh, it always seemed as though your English novelist couldn't make a fist even if they had the young, luscious Arthur Rimbaud bending over in front of them begging for it. Even the rather grungey Northern realist writers of the Sixties turned out to be putative Pansies, with a love of 'classical' music and 'fine' art which had turned them against their rank roots in the first place. But in the Seventies, with the influx of the *Granta* brigade, your average Oxbridge nance began yearning for a smaller vocabulary and a bigger pair of fongoolos; that's not to say he began boxing, going on three-day drinking binges and having brilliant, meaningful, *metaphorical* anal sex with beautiful, doomed, foreign women sweating perfect beads of pungent poetry, but that he began to *talk* about boxing, three-day drinking binges and having brilliant, meaningful, *metaphorical* anal sex with beautiful, doomed, foreign women sweating perfect beads of pungent poetry. Worse, he began to write about it.

But something was still missing. Sure, they had the pose and the prose down pat. But the plain brute *bigness* of the American boys was missing. Even boxing, bingeing and butt-fucking lost their existential anomie and started seeming as seedy and comforting as your grandma's stained nightdress when set in the British Isles rather than in the belly of the beast. For it is undeniable that the very word AMERICAN adds a non-specific epic grandeur to whatever title of book or play it is contained in: *An American Tragedy; American Heart; American Buffalo.* But send them for a spin round the block, or the world, and do I have any takers for *An Australian Tragedy, Holland Heart* or *Belgian Buffalo*? The literary lads of London could play as much pinball as they liked; when they looked in the mirror, the neon WANKER! still winked knowingly.

American novels were huge, and dealt with CIA conspiracy, military might, the quagmire of politics, an America wallowing in the mire of post-Vietnam trauma. In the Seventies English novels were still slim, and the general impression one gets from them was that their main beef was how awful it was that people dropped McDonalds cartons in the street. English novelists had rejected what they saw as the Musn't Grumble complacency of English life, but they had merely replaced it with a Must Grumble complacency. All through the Seventies and early Eighties, one feels that all the 'serious' novelists from Amis to Drabble are writing as swimmers with cramp tread water – hoping against hope they'll remember soon why they wanted to be writers in the first place.

And then it happened – on St Valentine's Day, as though Norman Mailer himself had written it. Mailer must have tied one on good and proper that night; the Big Fight at last, and they'd sent a Limey to do an American's job! The Big Idea, the Big Match, the Big Fight that literature had been searching for for the best part of a century happened on 14 February 1989; they'd been cruising for a bruising, and now Islam had offered them outside in the unsuspecting figure of Salman Rushdie.

Writers had always boasted of 'defending to the death' the right to free speech; the problem was that it was never the writers who said this who ended up defending *anything* to the death, but ordinary, conscripted Joes who had *never* made such rash promises. Now, all the tough talk would be put to the test.

Rushdie went into his corner – or rather, hiding – and came out swinging like a genuine contender: 'Secular versus religious, the light versus the dark. Better choose which side you are on.' He even sounded like Churchill at times: 'Now the battle has spread to Britain. It is time for us to choose.' We were ready to fight them in the bookshops, fight them in the lending libraries!

It was a phoney war of words to end them all; four weeks later, Rushdie offered an apology to the Iranian government, the very people who had put the assassination bounty on his head ('death sentence' gives the threat a dignity it has no right to), for the 'distress' *The Satanic Verses* had caused sensitive Muslims around the world. It came as a bit of a shock, like hearing Bomber Harris apologize for Dresden, but his supporters struggled on manfully. Anyway, by the February of 1990 it was the *paperback* that was on everyone's mind: a new stand, a new start.

Should it be published? 'Yes!' cried born-to-be-wild Martin Amis, this sap – sorry, *his* sap rising. 'Let the book be sold on street corners by Securicor . . .' (there they go again, some innocent blue-collar bystander corralled into defending something he neither understands nor approves of, to the death!) '. . . if need be; but we must do the right thing!' (How about *you* selling it on street corners, white boy?) 'Yes!' cried homeboy Hanif Kureishi. 'We must not be intimidated by Right-wing fundamentalism!' (As if Left-wing fundamentalism would have been fine and dandy!) 'Yes!' cried Salman himself, Diana to this Mary and Flo, 'Because if the paperback does not appear it will have been, in all practical terms, suppressed!'

On 25 September 1990, Salman Rushdie announced that he had abandoned plans for a paperback version of *The Satanic Verses*. He also told the world, apparently without shame, that he had become a Muslim.

Tellingly, it was an Un-Luvvy – the brilliant lawyer and scholar Francis Bennion – who reacted with horror and revulsion to this dazzling act of perfidy. Quite rightly he reasoned that a man who could convert to the very religion which thought it just to hand out death sentences for blasphemy, and had in fact declared one on himself, was no longer worthy of a liberal Western defence. In the February of this year, on the occasion of yet another *fatwa* anniversary and its inevitable accompanying breast-beating from the Friends of Rushdie, Mr Bennion wrote thus to the *Guardian*:

> Sickening, that hand-wringing by famous authors in your feature on the Rushdie *fatwa*. Just this sort of feebleness made me resign a year ago from the International Committee for the Defence of Salman Rushdie and his publishers.
>
> Paul Theroux remarks to Rushdie, 'The first step (after three years!) is for governments to speak out on your behalf. Then it is our turn – the writers and readers.' Nadine Gordimer says, 'How has world concern allowed the murderous edict against you to continue year after year?'
>
> The answer is simple. Rushdie's fellow authors, whom this issue most closely concerns, have not shown enough backbone. In fact they have shown no backbone at all.
>
> We in Britain are fortunate to live under a system that clearly says incitement to murder and conspiracy to murder are crimes, and gives every citizen a right to prosecute for them. When I tried to persuade the International Committee (largely composed of authors' representatives) to exercise its civil rights, I failed.
>
> I wanted the committee to set up a procedure to collect evidence. With that, I then wanted it to put pressure on the prosecuting authorities. If they failed to act, a private prosecution could be brought. The committee declined.
>
> That is why I am no longer a member of the committee and Mr Rushdie still languishes in hiding, without prospect of relief.

The writers had been acting all along as though they wanted the Big Match, in order to fight the Big Fight and put the Big Idea into practice; how was Mr Bennion, with his cool, clear mind to know they were just being Luvvies, pouting for the camera? After they'd lectured us endlessly on the need to 'do the right thing', on our 'moral duty' to defend the principle of free speech, their very moral centre – Rushdie – had reneged on the deal. And more or less to a man, the Luvvies came on like Tammy Wynette – stand by your Salman! 'I would rather betray my country than betray my friend' has a certain schmaltzy nobility; 'I would rather betray my moral principles than betray my friend' is the language of the rapist's loyal wife. It is language that denies that there is any such thing as society.

The Rushdie Affair was never about making a moral stand on the part of the Luvvies; it had never been a struggle between light and dark, which the Luvvies see as *Sun*-editorial simplification anyway. ('Things *are* black and white. They always were,' says Loren Estelman's gumshoe hero Amos Walker. 'The only people who think things are shades of grey are people who've had some of the black rub off on them.') It was just about the Luvvies of literature, no longer left on the bookshelf by the other celebrity squares but suddenly *sexy, most wanted, a matter of life and death*, putting on a show. And when Rushdie did yet another about turn, announced that he was no longer a Muslim and planned to bring out the paperback after all, the Luvvies rallied again, making speeches about issues of principle once more. It was like some joyous revival of a much-loved play – *Salman Days*.

This one, of course, will run and run, with Rushdie returning to the stage repeatedly in his best-loved role.

The *fatwa* anniversary will go down in the alternative social calendar, like holidays in Tuscany and days at Glyndebourne. And then it will be business – show business – as usual: the lunches, the launches, the indecent advances.

Every writer has a secret; the literary love that dare not speak its name. It's the mad wife in the attic and the hooker under the bed, and it's called having a career. And in the end the Big Career proved far more important than the Big Fight and the Big Idea, especially to Rushdie himself. The Rushdie Affair taught us many things, most importantly that multi-culturalism in a political sense – as opposed to Indian restaurants and supermarket soul food – is not only unlikely but undesirable, allowing as it does so many injustices of gender and caste which far outstrip the dirty little prejudices of the host society. One of the minor things it taught us is that the more a writer seems willing to go six rounds with Joe Louis for the sake of his art, the more he really wants to be alone pressing wild flowers – or at least his cuttings.

Writers are selfish people, with a love of their own company so passionate that it seems entirely likely that one day one of us just might get ourselves pregnant. And writers, except of the most prosaically political kind, do not write to confront big ideas, but to *avoid* them. This is probably why it is so difficult and embarrassing to write about writing: so many grandiose, vainglorious claims have been made on its behalf.

Writing is more than anything a compulsion, like some people wash their hands thirty times a day for fear of awful consequences if they do not. It pays a whole lot better than this type of compulsion, but it is no more heroic. You are either born with a love of words and what they can do, or you are not.

Born into a bookless house, books became my religion around the age of ten; I accepted this as a compulsion, and certainly nothing heroic, and got on with life. As an impossibly jaded thirteen-year-old, a smoker, drinker, shoplifter and all-round trainee cherry bomb, I ran into a pair of the toughest girls in my peer group one Saturday morning on my way back from the library. They had been there earlier too, they said, which surprised me, and they'd stolen a book, which didn't. (Big deal – I did it all the time.) *But then they took out the book, and proceeded to rip huge fistfuls of pages out of it!*

Then they offered it to me; it was some sort of sorority test, to see if I could make the inner sanctum. I remember well what happened. I literally *snarled* at them, my Plum Gone lips curling back from my baby teeth. I've never seen two people who weren't actually competing in a major running event move so fast. They dropped the book at my feet; I picked it up. It was dead dramatic.

From that day on, my name was mud with the J.D. set – and naturally I wasn't going to hang around with no *nerds*. That bloody book – something smug by Pat Smythe – marked me for life: I was an outcast, the Salman Rushdie of Somerset! But I never felt persecuted, or heroic, that was just the way things were. 'Take what you want, and pay for it, says God' is a Spanish proverb; I wanted words. Any price was worth paying.

It is the pathetic over-compensatory and cod-political heroics of male writers which have made me embarrassed to call myself by the name. In future, to alleviate this distressing condition, might it be possible to say more about the *honour* of being able to write, and less about the honour we do others by allowing them to read us? Can we talk, and write, less about the manly courage writing requires, and more about the rewards it yields? Can we stop comparing it to working down a coalmine, and admit that it is far more like walking a tightrope, an altogether more feminine and finicky business? If you're lucky, you get from one side to another.

But if you're really lucky, you fall off.

And you fly.

SEX

WHERE'S THE BEEF?
OR WHY ALL MEN ARE NOT
CREATED EQUAL

. . . .

'Those English girls, they do love a big
cock. Size queens, we call them.'
Andy Warhol to Fiona Russell Powell

The bodies which women were born with, from the
Rokeby Venus to the Goude Grace, have always been
the slaves of male taste and artistic whim. The ideal
woman must not have feet of clay – but it will be better
for her popularity if she has breasts, hips and lips of clay;
all the easier to cut down and build up with the changing
trend.

It has always been men who have judged and shaped
the wild contradictory ideas of beauty that women feel
compelled to live up to. Many of these image-makers are
misogynist, homosexual or both; a leader in the field, a
stylist feared beyond all others, asked a friend of mine,
'What's it like being a woman – walking around like a
big open wound?' Unfortunately, she didn't ask him how
it felt to walk around like an itsy-bitsy teeny-weeny
cocktail sausage.

It is to such men that the image of women is entrusted.
Yet no one questions the motives of these men whose

whole *raison d'être* seems at times to be how to make the largest number of women feel inadequate in order to take revenge for *their* inadequacy, the biggest one of all – that of not being born a woman. If you can't join them, beat them – or at least get them to wear puffball skirts, thus eliminating whatever allure they may have possessed.

Whereas blacks who bleach their skin are seen as self-loathing traitors to their race, women who undergo medical mutilation are not perceived as being in any way sick. The breast is currently the most pathologized part of the female body; in both aesthetic and medical terms, breasts are a *problem* first and foremost. Between the Cancer Police dragging women from shopping malls in order to subject them to Nanny State's screening programmes, and the designers dictating how many inches you need off *this* season, the human breast has less chance than any other part of the body bar the teeth of going to the grave intact. Interestingly, one of the most unappealing words of recent years has been 'boob', denoting a breast, a mistake or an embarrassment. That a slang word for the penis might also denote a mistake or an embarrassment is unthinkable. (Though much more accurate, some would say.)

The shaving down (Dido Goldsmith) or the pumping up (Mariel Hemingway) of the breast has made a million men millionaires. Even more than public breast-feeding, cosmetic surgery has rendered the breast a public property, a family affair, with very little left to mystery and imagination. In a riotous story of American mores, Sylvester Stallone's mother first found her daughter-in-law with another woman (and it wasn't the Avon Lady) when she went over to the house to help Brigitte choose her new silicone implant by way of a gesture of reconciliation. Just like picking out wallpaper.

No part of the female body escapes the schizoid scrutiny of meat à la mode. Behinds: one decade Monroe, the next Twiggy – try performing *that* miracle of deflation. Hips – from La Lollo to the Shrimp. The blonde bimbo and the brunette vamp have been played off against each other since Pickford and Bara. Even mouths can't make up their minds where to draw the line; Clara's bow or Nastassja's overbite? Surgery and silicone, liposuction and lipstick, diet and dye – all the sleight of hand that carvery and cosmetics can manage make the modern Eve, occasionally with tragic results. Everyone knows someone who knows someone who's gone into the clinic looking a couple of pounds overweight and come out looking like they've been in a five-car pile-up on the M1.

Men, even in the meat markets of entertainment, do not face the same pressures. The rules are so different that even that which is unattractive – Woody Allen's skinniness, Dustin Hoffman's dwarfism, Bruce Willis' chrome dome syndrome – are rallied and re-interpreted as 'off-beat' sexiness. Men alter perceptions to accommodate their basic features; women alter *themselves*. It's the difference between self-defence and suicide.

Every bad thing that can befall a man has been thoughtfully kitted out with a safety net of its own; no wonder they fly through the air with the greatest of ease. Keep taking the tabloids: Why Bald Men Are Sexy, Why Ugly Men Are Sexy, Why Old Men Are Sexy. Men are judged as the sum of their parts while women are judged as some of their parts; men are judged as an entity, and their failings alchemized into trademarks, while women are judged in hard cold feet and inches. Men have charisma; women have vital statistics.

But just as supposedly invulnerable men have the biggest Achilles ache of all between their legs, they also keep there the secret of a statistic more vital than any measurement a woman, even a flat-chested or thick-ankled woman, could have: the size of the penis. More than any other part of the body the penis can be judged good or bad, adequate or deficient; because, much more so than the hips and lips of a woman, it actually has a job to do and a gap to bridge. It is not just there to look pretty, a thing it is very bad at anyway. A joy forever is not *always* a thing of beauty.

And considering the merciless scrutiny to which their bodies have been subjected down the centuries, it really is time that women – who have always been too nice for their own good, especially in the sack – took the gloves off (or more specifically the English Gloves, as the French call the condom) and had a good hard look at what's inside. Because there you will find the most vital statistic of all.

In recent years, since the so-called sexual revolution – a licence to print funny money if ever there was one – there has been a great deal of stress laid by liberal sexperts on the idea that penis size is unimportant. As with most liberal sexual ideas, what makes the world a better place for men invariably makes it a duller and more dangerous place for women – prostitution, pornography and 'no fault' divorce. The myth of all penises being equal is another one; started, I can only conclude, by a sexologist who had the misfortune to be hung like a hamster.

Technique, not size, is what matters, goes the line. But after three decades of this accepted wisdom, 98 per cent of women interviewed by Shere Hite declared themselves 'disappointed' with heterosex. If all men are equal, and technique can be learned, why should this be so? The answer is probably that 98 per cent of American men have a small penis. And the fact is that once the kissing and foreplay are over, what's left in the bed is the three of you – the boy, the girl and the beef. 'Technique' making everything swoony is a condescending idea which implies that women can be taken in by a bit of fumbling around on a man's part; what's worse it makes numerous women feel abnormal when endless fiddling around doesn't do anything for them.

The denial of the importance of size by the male medical establishment is just another brick in the wall of male ego-armour, and has done absolutely nothing for the sex lives of women. On the contrary, it has given them yet another sexual failure to take the blame for; if any sized penis will do the trick, it must be *my* fault I don't feel anything.

Rubbish. Show me a frigid woman and, nine times out of ten, I'll show you a little man. Face it; every girl wants one, and every man does too; no one, given the chance, would *choose* the small model. If it's so good, why is the dildo industry built on twelve-inchers? Why do pop stars stuff handkerchiefs down their trousers rather than bind down the offending object? And why are condoms never marked Small, Medium and Large but Large, Jumbo and Super Jumbo? Because instinct admits to what indoctrination cannot swallow.

How big is big? More than eight inches. More than eleven can be problematic. But not half as problematic as less than seven! All men and women with the sense they were born with know this, despite thirty years of Establishment bleating to the contrary. Whenever the

Playboy Advisor Page ran short of letters, it would only need to make up one along the lines of 'Mine is twelve inches, but my girlfriend says this is too small' for the sackloads of begging letters to flood in – letters from men *begging* to be told that they were big enough.

The penis is mightier than the sword of Damocles when it comes to hanging over men's heads threatening to puncture their sense of self with every step towards the bed they take. Their obsession, far too heavy for them to carry alone, has been pushed on to the shoulders of women, blacks and other beasts of burden since the year dot. But the myth of penis envy has no grounding in fact; I have never met a woman who contemplated the extension without a degree of horror. As a Verity Bargate heroine says when asked by her leering Freudian analyst if she has ever wanted a penis: 'No, because it might be a small one. And men tend to worry a lot about that.'

The proof is in the cuttings on the plastic surgeon's floor; since the first sex-change in 1952 on the American GI George Jorgenson, there have been hundreds of thousands of male to female operations. But not until 1977 was the first female to male sex-change performed on a Missouri student, and less than a hundred have followed. It is not women who suffer from penis envy but *men* who, when not kidding themselves that women want to be like them, are tormenting themselves with the idea that the 'inferior' races are hung like *übermensch*.

Racist literature, such as it is, from the Ku Klux Klan to the British Movement, spends an unnaturally long time brooding over the sexual desires and capacities of its *bête noire*.

Clever black men exploit the legend. Jack Johnson, the first black heavyweight champion of the world, was the first black celebrity – dying in 1946 – to act like a Black rather than a Negro, and his penis was his favourite blunt instrument with which to whiten Whitey's hair. In his silk suits and Stutz Bearcat he rode around Chicago with his white girl and white wine sipped through solid gold straws, even playing Othello. When he said, 'I can get any white woman I want,' one hundred Texans arrived in a lynch party.

Rioting whites, every time Johnson knocked out a white man or knocked up a white woman, caused the deaths of nineteen people in seven years. Johnson was unrepentant; hearing white talk of his 'gigantic, over-sized thing', he laughed and wrapped yards of gauze bandages around it, parading around the ring in the skin-tight trunks of the day. (N.B. Loose boxer shorts as we know them were introduced shortly afterwards.)

The great white hope these days is that the racists were wrong and that black men are the same as 'us' (white men, as 'us' always is). The black stars of today are effete or asexual to a fault – Murphy, Prince, Jackson. Millie Jackson has a routine about how bad black men are in bed while Richard Pryor has a joke about alleged black longevity – 'We can't go all night. *I* can't. I can go for two minutes, and then I need a bowl of Wheatiechomps and eight hours sleep.' No wonder the white boys love him. White girls, however, have yet to be convinced; some years ago a leading London model agency took an informal poll of its girls' sexual tastes. Black men won by a nose. Or something.

As black men were once slaves to whites, now white men are slaves to their genitalia. Only they will never be free. Female sex symbols are shown in gloating biographies as being in a constant state of anxiety over the size and shape of their breasts from the minute they hit the wrong side of twenty-two. Big deal; a good 90 per cent of men worry about the size and shape of *their* equipment from the age of twelve till the day they die.

The tensions in this silent war of self-loathing constantly erupt. The murder of women by men they are married to or live with is now running at more than two a week, usually over some alleged sexual slur. The husband of a flat-chested woman can drool over Linda Lusardi eight days a week, and if she killed him for it she'd be awarded a one-way ticket to Broadmoor in the great lottery of life. But let a woman disparage a cohabiting penis, and she can be killed on the spot by its owner while *he* gets away with a suspended sentence – they call it a crime of passion when what they mean is a crime of temper tantrum. She 'taunted' him, the defence invariably say.

Pretending that all men are born equal has done nothing to quell their sexual neuroses; sex crimes of all sorts, from indecent exposure to incest, are on the eternal up. So why shouldn't we at least enjoy the luxury of telling the truth? Which is that the small penis is the mourner at every wedding and the time bomb in every bed, ready to have its pin pulled and its bluff called by a cross word at any minute.

But it's not their fault! soft-hearted, half-witted Earth Mothers will bleat. Well no; but is it any woman's fault that she's a 32B in a culture which worships Kathy Lloyd?

If women can take the rap for the bodies they are born with, so can men, the sensitive little blossoms. Until then, until they learn to say what they want, women are going to have to like what they get. Time to take the gloves off – and hit below the belt.

Big

Charles II	
Toulouse-Lautrec	A hump and a half.
Rasputin	Thirteen inches. Lucky for some!
Milton Berle	Approached by a drunk in a New York bath house: 'Hey, Berle! I hear you've got a big one! A hundred dollars if it's bigger than mine!' Mr Berle revealed only three-quarters of what was beneath his towel; the drunk paid and fled.
Gary Cooper	'Not only good on a horse but hung like one,' said Clara Bow.
Conrad Hilton and his two sons	'A yard of cock between us.'
Jim Kerr	'How does Jim Kerr get his cock to be twelve inches?' 'He folds it in half.' It's no coincidence that Simple Minds can only play stadiums these days.
Frank Sinatra	When asked what it was like being married to a 120-pound runt, Ava Gardner replied, 'Great! Because there's only 10 pounds of Frank and 110 pounds of cock!'

Buddy Holly	Little Richard said he packed a foot, and it didn't have toenails either! That'll be the day, indeed!

Small

King Farouk	
Nijinsky	
Napoleon Bonaparte	Under one inch at time of death.
Montgomery Clift	They called him Princess Tiny Meat!
Scott Fitzgerald	Told by Zelda that 'due to a matter of measurements' he could never satisfy a woman, he consulted Hemingway who pronounced him 'normal'. Included though by virtue of two unreliable witnesses; mistress Sheilah Graham's back-handed compliment, 'Given the choice between a donkey and a chipmunk, I choose the chipmunk,' and because . . .
Ernest Hemingway	Was not the best judge of these things. 'Of course, his big problem was that he was worried by the size of it' – holding up little finger of left hand, thumbnail at the base –

'About the size of a thirty-thirty shell'. Testimony of Sidney Franklin, alleged best friend.

Liars

Norman Mailer

Wrote about 'my modest Jewish dick'. DON'T BELIEVE IT. As the most magnificently endowed race of all – see marriage choices of all great sex queens from Monroe, Taylor and Mansfield to Welch, Evans and Principal – a 'modest' little Jewish number weighs in at around nine and a half inches.

THE PHANTOM NYMPHO RIDES AGAIN

. . . .

Just like a desert shows a thirsty man
A green oasis where there's only sand
You lured me into something I should have dodged
The love I saw in you was just a mirage

(Smokey Robinson/Marvin Tarplin)

She's back. I really thought I'd seen the back of her, visible pantyline and all; that her ashes were safely scattered throughout the chalky, sulky lockers of my schooldaze. Put away forever with other childish souvenirs of a blood royal white working-class early-Seventies girlhood, like two-tone Trevira suits, 'Double Barrel' and *Lift Off With Ayesha*. I never *dreamed* she'd turn up *now*, of all modern times, when men are supposed to be so . . . new. But here she is – large as life and twice as louche.

Looka there! – is it a girl? Is it a, *sorry*, woman? NO – IT'S THE PHANTOM NYMPHO! And she's *raring* to go, as per! Like King Arthur, see, she wasn't really dead; just sleeping (around) till her people felt in need of her once more. And now she's back. BACK!

And *still* wearing those to-die-for white slingbacks, I see . . .

NYMPHO – now there's a beautiful sunlit Seventies word for you, redolent of that brief shining second of sexual freedom *after* the smelly hippies stopped giving It a bad name but *before* big diseases with little names. It expressed all the lewd, eager innocence of the young Richard Beckinsdale sitting on a sit-com sofa and trying to get Paula Wilcox to come across on it.

No chance; *she* wasn't a nympho, worse luck, but a fiancée, and thus given to referring to the dirty deed as 'Percy Filth'. But somewhere – you could tell by the never-say-die gleam in his eye – Richard just *knew* there was a nympho with his name on. As there was for every likely lad lucky enough to find his place in the *Sun* in the Seventies; the last (one night) stand of safe sex.

In the Seventies the alleged sexual revolution of the Sixties hit prime-time mainstream with a nudge, a wink and a nympho. Stripped of the phoney rhetoric about being a powerful tool of social insurrection (there's no limit to what ugly hippies who want to get laid will say to a girl; they leave Iberian waiters – 'If only I were worthy to be the father of your children!' – standing), sex stood cheerfully akimbo, sportif and ready for action. The tennis player scratching her BTM was the perfect icon of the age (Betjeman Girl Meets Bond Girl – Love All!); the sexy, snazzy, jazzy novels of Molly Parkin the perfect fast flick between fast fucks. That which had been dark and dangerous since the first time in the primeval slime became cheap and cheerful overnight. Deregulation, irreverance and undress, test-driven by the underground, saw the light of day in the Seventies, when mammaries met Mammon in family newspapers.

But even then, especially on prime-time, your actual *nympho* proved somewhat elusive. Richard O'Sullivan, sideburns sweating, endlessly chased girls he imagined in his wettest, wildest dreams were nymphos – usually played by Jenny Hanley, Françoise Pascal and Luan Peters, not flirting but drowning in a sea of dusky pink suede espadrilles, velveteen hotpants and sticky brown cheekbone shader – through 'bachelor pads' that looked disappointingly like one's parents' front room. But being a sit-com dickhead, he'd usually got the wrong end of the stick and they weren't really nymphos at all; just girls-next-door in drag. Fade out over laughter across a trattoria trough for two . . .

Still, in pursuit of said Phantom Nympho, much fun had been had – and more *entendres* doubled than you could shake a stick at. And there was always *next* week. That was the thing about the nympho; like *The Fugitive*'s one-armed man, she was always *just around the corner*. Like the pantomime villain – *behind you!* But next time she'd be for real.

Nympho was, and still is, one of the very few *cheerful* words to do with sex, the lexicon of which reads as though conceived by a constipated Kraut with a mother fixation. It lacks the fatalistic contempt of *slag*, the prole self-loathing of *scrubber*, the overblown Mafia melodrama of *whore*. It long ago left behind the name it was born with – *'Nymphomania: a feminine disease characterized by morbid and uncontrollable sexual desire'*, *OED* – hinting as it did at all sorts of something-nasty-in-the-woodshed murkiness, and gave itself a new, gimmicky handle to go with its showbizzy aspirations. Lulu – Twinkle – Twiggy – NYMPHO!

Feminists are supposed to hate all the names men have for women – I have a dictionary in which *broad*, *sheila* and *ducky* are all categorized as terms of abuse – but there really is a good deal of difference between them. 'A bit of skirt' is nothing more than the female counterpart of the phrase beloved of Cockney girls, 'a bit of trouser', and there's no use pretending otherwise. In my part of Somerset, men and women of my parents' generation used the word 'tart' to signify a young woman who inspired affection in one, especially a daughter or grand-daughter. If you had pointed out that the word held connotations of prostitution, they would have given you a punch up the bracket.

My favourite word for a sexually generous girl has always been *goer*, as in 'a bit of a goer' and 'she really goes' – always spoken with a note of yearning admiration as though the dame in question was a whippet, a racehorse or a jaguar of higher or lower case, but always a thoroughbred. The difference between being a goer and a slag is comparable to the difference between having a suntan and melanoma.

A good part of the reason why *nympho* is so inoffensive is the stress it puts on the *active* role of the named one; it was always an important part of the legend that a nympho would just knock you down and tear your clothes off – *you* didn't have to do a thing. Her Seventies prototype was Valerie Leon, the Hai Karate Amazon (the Seventies being the big decade of alleged aphrodisiacs, guaranteed to turn even Paula Wilcox into a *raving nympho*) who took one whiff of Mr Nobody's aftershave and pursued him through Egyptology before pushing him into an open casket, climbing in on top of him and pulling the lid down. *Cor!*

It seems to me that the accepted notion that women want to be courted and seduced — now finding favour with ageing swingers and feminists, even — is far more patronizing than the Hai Karate commercial ever was, and less amusing. And more importantly, far more likely to lead to misunderstandings and violence of the type filed manageably away in the category Date-Rape — the very word seduction implying as it does an *overcoming* by one party of the *natural reluctance* of the other. But you can't seduce a nympho.

So it was always the *sweeter* sort of boy who used the word, one not particularly interested in the tired old Me Tarzan, You Chased/Chaste routine; the boy who didn't really care *who* was on top so long as he got laid. Callow, clumsy, but reasonably clean-limbed and clear-consciensed, and above all *hopeful*, he was the eternal optimist who might have been going steady with his harem comprising Mrs Fist and her five daughters since he was in short trousers, but remained confident that it was only a *temporary* blip. *Because next week he'd meet a nympho — no, a RAVING nympho — and she'd see him all right!*

And you know what? He was right.

Suddenly in the second half of the Seventies, you stopped hearing the word. For a very simple reason. If everyone is doing it, then *no one is a nympho.* Phantom no longer, she now existed only in Whitehall farces, and in the minds of the middle-aged men in the audience who *still* weren't getting any.

The Seventies were, of course, the great decade of Lad

– and the nympho was nothing if not Lad's anima, his muse, his sparring partner in the great mud-wrestling competition of life. The Seventies was one big Stringfellow's – one big easy. But with the onset and the mindset of the Eighties, something happened.

The nympho next door and the Lad on the Clapham omnibus saw their idols fall one by one: Bestie, Rodders, Barry Sheene, John Conteh, bettered by bailiffs and blondes every one. The sunset of *Playboy*; the motherhood of Fiona Richmond; the taming of Marji Wallace (Miss World Goes Nympho!); the end of the *Confessions* and *Carry On* films (for two decades the British film industry was based entirely on the promise that all housewives were really nymphos): they all drove a nail into the coffin of nympho-normalization.

And women changed, too. Gradually, they stopped behaving like nymphos – which paved the way, of course, for the return of the Phantom. The new Thatcherite feminist refused to be sexually blackmailed by men, whereas socialist feminists had been such a pushover legover – 'Do it for the Grunwick pickets!'

A first-time surplus of young men (a million in Britain alone) meant that women were no longer strutting their stuff in a buyers' market – none of that 'Sleep with me by Saturday or I'll shag your sister on Sunday' rubbish any more, thank you. And then there was AIDS, which stopped sex from being 'just like shaking hands' (popular Seventies simile) and made it marginally more like kissing Death. All in all, sex became *serious* in the Eighties, no longer a lark or a giggle. In the Seventies you couldn't have made a film which treated one night of nooky as a matter of life and death; in the Eighties, you could make *Fatal Attraction*, in which sex was pathologized to an extent not seen on the screen since *Repulsion*, twenty-two years earlier.

Sex has been re-pathologized. And just like in 1963, when every night at the drive-in saw Warren Beatty pleading with Natalie Wood to give him a bit of what he fancied before he flipped his lid (*Splendor in the Grass* really *did* posit the notion that lack of sex could actually drive a man certifiably insane – Warren Beatty, maybe), sex starvation among single men is back. This is the first era since the end of the Second World War when married men are getting more sex than single ones; *that's* how bad it is.

In the Sixties everyone talked about sex; in the Seventies everyone did it *and* talked about it. In the Eighties they still did it, though not half as much, and they talked about it less, too. Now they've gone back to talking – talking and hallucinating. Yes, the Phantom Nympho rides again; and this time, sightings have risen alarmingly not just among clammy schoolboys but among thirtysomethings with Double Firsts.

But this time the game, as well as the stalker, wears a different disguise. The Phantom Nympho used to be your standard sex kitten: young, blonde, compliant. But over the years the fact has sunk in – albeit reluctantly – that lots of beautiful girls (especially those exhibiting nympho tendencies) are actually rather revolted by sex. From Marilyn to Mandy, we share their suffering – and that takes the fun, the *innocence*, out of it. Nymphos, more than any other type of girl, should *enjoy* it.

So in a new twist on an old chestnut, Phantom Nympho Nouveau isn't a shook-up teenage starlet, looking for love in a looking-glass world, but a *dragon*. The last one you imagined it of: the strong, self-motivated control freak. *That's* Nineties Nympho Nouveau.

———

Over the past six months, I have heard from numerous sources sworn testaments of the raving nymphohood of the following: the stern, school-marmy newsreader; the brisk, bossy MP; the robust Royal; Elena Ceauşescu. There is a double advantage in believing such women are nymphos: *(a)* they obviously haven't been *forced* into it like poor Marilyn, they've just got to have it! And *(b)* it's so far-fetched – strange but true! – that if *she* can be one, any woman can be one! Ipso facto, *I won't be jerking off much longer, please God!*

The Phantom Nympho has come full circle-jerk. But does she still exist in the flesh, outside of rumour, wet dream and the books of Martin Amis (a man incapable of writing women who are anything but nymphos; his 'strongest' woman, he claims, is Nicola Six, a thirty-six-year-old failed actress who wears frilly underwear and wants to be murdered – by a *man*, natch. Good God, what is his *weakest* female character like?)? Jammy Pammy Bordes made several nympho-spotting hearts beat faster (it was the amyl nitrate that did it), but a girl who does it for money rarely does it for fun; prostitution has that unmistakable ring of sadness about it, no matter how many Chanel handbags it hides its shame in. In the end Pamella's first concern was fiscal, not physical, pleasure; and in the nympho stakes, just like the Olympics, you get disqualified for being a professional. The nympho is by nature a creature of furtive, fleeting word of mouth, and cannot be proven flesh or fantasy. All that can be said for sure is that the name is back. It would be a shame to think this an unqualified Bad Thing.

Some feminists forget that slander, like Amex, says more about you than money ever can. They get cross about so-called sexist language when they ought to see that, like a boomerang, it goes flying back to he who dealt it. Thus men who are desperate for career success call achieving women 'Thatcherite bitches'; men who aren't getting fucked call women 'slags'. All the return of the Phantom Nympho proves is that men are going without sex in great numbers once more. And giving women, as this does, the chance to call the shots, this can only be a good thing.

So let us not sermonize and sulk; let us not miserabilize and moan. Let us instead read between the lines, and decode their dirty minds. And let us crack open a bottle of Bolly, and drink to the Phantom Nympho; our sister under the skintrade.

THE DEAD ZONE:
THE RISE OF THE RELATIONSHIP
AND THE DEATH OF ROMANCE

. . . .

In a recent TV commercial, a fresh-faced, beatifically boring young couple walk home through the rain to their dream house, flagrantly flaunting their heterosexuality for all they're worth. It could be an ad for a building society, a chain of pizza takeaways or even, things being what they are, a condom.

But no. What it really is is an attempt to flog you a series of magazines called *One To One*. In the same way that people were once encouraged to build up a useless library of data on cookery and crochet, collected week by week and stuffed into genuine imitation leather binders, they are now being sold a series on *relationships*. One to one, geddit?

Relationships of what type we do not know, but judging from the relentless normality of the commercial it is fair to say that troilism, tribadism and trisexuality (as in 'I'll tri anything once!') are not likely to get much of a look in.

Relationship. The word itself is reasonable, tolerant — and singularly unsexy. People who have relationships put the kettle on, talk things out and 'grow'. In other words, they behave like Stepford Wives. People who have *affairs*, on the other hand, have violent sexual intercourse and fist fights. In other words, they behave like human beings.

Before relationships, men and women (as opposed to 'people' – another big blandspeak buzzword) had flings, quick ones, dirty weekends and marriages. If they wanted a relationship, they had it with their mother or a friend of the same sex. But now the whole dizzying and delirious range of sexual possibilities has been boiled down to that one big, boring, bulimic word. RELATIONSHIP.

Once again, class, we may safely lay the blame at the chipped and peeling door of the Sixties, right next to the over-ordered milk of human kindness which has curdled to a bitter shade of bile. The whole naive crusade to take the dirt out of sex – which is a little like taking the taste out of food – really threw the baby out with the patchouli-scented bathwater. Sex was *meant* to be dirty, dangerous and disturbing. It wasn't meant to leave you feeling good about yourself; this is the fatal mistake that the relationship merchants made.

In the Fifties women had figures and men had physiques, and pretty damn good they looked to each other too. Since the Sixties we have all had 'bodies' (Gina Lollobrigida had a figure; Victor Mature had a physique; but Meryl Streep and Charles Dance both have bodies), a creepy word redolent of morgues and marble slabs. Even the condom has been castrated; once terminally nudge-nudge wink-wink sleazy, they are now called cosy, coy things like 'Mates'. Excuse my French, but condoms were meant to be called things like 'Thrust' and 'Whopper' – 'Mates' sounds like a teen magazine. In the Fifties, youngbloods drank the lethal martini; now they drink the bloodless spritzer. And the relationship is the spritzer of sex: weak, watered down and devoid of kicks.

'My mother said you kept a man by being a chef in the kitchen, a servant in the sitting room and a whore in the bedroom,' says Jerry Hall. 'I told her I'd make enough money to hire a cook and a maid and take care of the rest myself.' What the relationship goldrush has ignored is the fact that most healthy, mature adults do not want a nurturing mother/father figure at home – but a whore, of either sex. And if their partner (another horrid Relationspeak buzzword, making one think of law firms) won't be one, they'll go out and find someone who is.

One of the most sinister aspects of *Fatal Attraction* was its insistence on the 'happiness' of the marriage at its centre. The fact is that happily married men don't sleep around. What the couple have is a *relationship* par excellence; their *marriage* is lousy. This is often the combination these days though there are exceptions. A man married to a marvellous but maddening girl says, 'I have a great marriage – the sex, the fun – it's the best I've ever had. But our relationship is awful. I tell her my problems and she falls asleep.'

But how much better, and safer, than the alternative. He may need to call the Samaritans, but he won't have to go to a bimbo. And no one has as yet caught AIDS from a telephone. The point is that relationships you can get in many places; a marriage you can only have with one person at a time.

In *Fatal Attraction*, Anne Archer's Beth is understanding, supportive and such an all-round Wonderful Poisson that sleeping with her must be like drowning in molasses. You can't blame the poor jerk she's married to for taking a flyer with Glenn Close who, playing a

knife-wielding psychobimbo, must come like a breath of
fresh carbon monoxide after all that merciless mothering.
The wife is so busy having a relationship with her
husband that she forgets to have an affair with him; Alex
has been told by too many magazines that to have sex
with someone is automatically to have a relationship with
them. Both women, the man *and* the marriage are the
victims of the relentless emphasis on the relationship as
the cure for all ills and insecurities.

So who's to blame? Contrary to liberal belief, the only
way a society may achieve mental health is to apportion
blame for every crime and seek out the culprit with twelve
good men and true and a blowtorch. It's the fault of the
Sixties, for trying to detonate the sex bomb and pulling
out the wrong pin. It's the fault of the counselling
industry which has made even the most contented of
people feel that their growth is being stunted – even
EastEnders Michelle speaks in psychobabble at times: 'I've
got to find meself! I've got to grow!' – if they're not
engaged in the process of washing their dirty linen in
front of a paid professional twice a week.

The cult of the relationship can be seen as the
privatization of psychiatry – 'community care', as in
turning the mentally ill out from hospitals to bed and
breakfasts to walk the streets all day, or in this case to
bend the ear of the unfortunate spouse until the cows
come home. More women than men are currently paying
for analysis, backing up that much-believed line that
many girls only sleep with men so that the men will talk
to them afterwards. Shrinks can be said to fulfil the role
for women that prostitutes play for men; supplying the
real need without the time-consuming trimmings.

But to some extent, one has to blame the sexual politics

of feminism for the rise of the relationship. The logical and righteous influence of feminism, with the scales of justice in one hand and a newly-whetted Sabatier filleting knife in the other, is desirable in most spheres of life from the workplace to the law court. But there are some things which should not be subject to righteous logic, and sex is one of them.

Feminists believe that heterosex must be re-created as a vehicle of gentleness, of touch and embrace. That is, feminism seeks to turn the biggest, bloodiest carnivore in the world – passion – into a right-on cud-chewing vegan.

It can never work. Sex was never meant to be that way. Sex, on the whole, was meant to be short, nasty and brutish. If what you want is cuddling, you should buy a puppy. No one has yet said it better for women who *don't* want sex to be a close cousin of the warm bath than Amber Hollibaugh, the American feminist:

> Who are all the women who don't know yet what they like but intend to find out; who practice consensual S/M; like to sweat and talk dirty, see expressions of need sweep across their lovers' faces; are confused and need to experiment with their own idea of passion; are into power?

It is a misogynist truism that in the Seventies, men, especially in America, became homosexual *en masse* because women became aggressive and masculine on discovering feminism. It only takes a couple of braincells to rub together to work out that this isn't so. The men those men then proceeded to turn to were not smooth-skinned young transvestites but moustachioed, leather replicas of themselves, hence the American homosexual word 'clones'. Men don't go out and pick up a cowboy because they're scared of masculinity. They LOVE masculinity.

What feminism did, as its name suggests, was not to masculinize women but to ultra-feminize them. Before feminism, the young urban women of the Fifties and Sixties appeared tough and capable, sex partners without tears, to the young men they worked, met and slept with. Post-feminism, the very state of being a woman was pathologized; even fat was a feminist issue. Women's problems were suddenly public property as the state of their wombs, breasts and hormone levels were broadcast on everything from TV-AM to Radio 4.

Post-feminism, women were born again as seething volcanoes of cancers, complexes and complaints. And a good deal of these are about sex; every American sex book published, from Kinsey to Hite, stresses women's need to be 'cuddled' and their distress at being 'used' by over-enthusiastic men. As if it wasn't as impossible to have good sex without using as it is possible to eat without chewing! It sometimes seems that modern women desire some toothless mutant of sex that slips down like babyfood with the minimum of mastication (maybe they think it makes you go blind).

This is the point: one thing which I do believe has contributed to the gay exodus of men is the ultra-feminization of sex.

If women insist on killing sex with kindness, that is their right. But if they insist on completely overruling the nature of male sexuality, they may find themselves getting their tactile satisfaction from their pillow while men are off brutalizing each other. In recent years, young women have been complaining about the man shortage, *despite* – and this is the interesting bit – the fact that young men vastly outnumber young women in this country. There are thought to be twenty *thousand* leftover men in London alone. There should be a male *smorgasbord*. There *is*. But they're doing it with each other.

By domesticating sex, we do not encourage monogamy but promiscuity. The human animal is very prone to needing to take a walk on the wild side every so often, and if she/he has a big brother/earth mother waiting at home as opposed to a sex object, they're much more likely to go out and do the dirty deed with a complete stranger.

Men and women should have sex, not relationships. Relationships are a saccharine substitute for sex; you have them with people you don't really fancy. They're a consolation prize in the big hoopla of life. Sexually involved people should return to the time when they were something in the way of strangers to each other, alien, foreign and a little bit frightening. If they could, adultery might decrease rapidly. The thrill of adultery, as anyone will tell you, is often the lure of the unknown, the new, the *other* rather than of an actual *improvement* in physical sex. And why do you need to chase a stranger, when you've got one at home?

KISS AND SELL

. . . .

'Anything worth doing is worth doing in public,' said Joe Orton. And for two generations of blondes from the Phyllosan sex-kitten Britt Ekland to the teenage phoenix in blue jeans Mandy Smith, things too rude to be done in public have received the next best attention. Kiss and tell has become kiss and sell.

A mere trickle in the Seventies, the confession business has become a deluge, as much the meat of popular publishing as the Royal Family. Being famous for fifteen minutes has undergone a subtle change; now, to *sleep* with someone famous for fifteen minutes (or five times a night in Fiona Wright's case) can lead to a whole new career of your own.

In a climate where everyone is encouraged to be their own creation and to exploit themselves for all they are worth, these young women have become the Typhoid Marys of capitalism. Men hate them; more privileged women sneer at them. Said Kim Wilde, 'I'm not a sleazy person, and I think it's so sad when you see girls selling their confessions to the tabloids. It's so pathetic that they can sell their private lives and I don't think some of them realize how they've prostituted themselves and what a valuable thing they're giving away. Maybe they value their Rive Gauche jackets more – they wouldn't give *those* away.'

This is a merciless judgement from a beautiful and intelligent young woman who not only cannot sing any better than Mandy Smith or Emma Ridley (but did happen to have a useful surname, unlike them) but who has exploited her singular physical gifts in a long line of explicitly sexy videos *and* has the safety net of a sturdy middle-class education to fall into should her records stop selling in sizeable quantities (as, indeed, there are signs they are doing already). Kiss-and-sell girls squeal for the same reason young black men box: there is nothing else that pays more than loose change that they are equipped for in life. For those with both careers and educations to dismiss them as human flotsam reveals a chilling lack of common humanity and a very fair helping of pomposity.

And no man would appear to have less of one and more of the other than the thinking man's *maître d'* Bryan Ferry, the conspicuous absence of whose most recent single 'Kiss And Tell' from the charts is a welcome change. Concerning the vileness of young female consorts of the rich and famous who spill the beans at the end of the affair, the accompanying video starred both Mandy Smith and Christine Keeler – a delicious and typical titbit of hypocrisy which proved, as if we needed reminding, that Mr Ferry is not above a little sexploitation himself.

The poignancy of the song and the singer's plight was not without cause. Mr Ferry has to date been involved with at least four women who have sold their tales of whoopee and woe to publishers and periodicals, these being Kari Ann Moller (also had: Keith Richard, Chris Jagger), Marilyn Cole (Victor Lownes, Hugh Hefner),

Amanda Lear (Salvador Dali, David Bowie) and Jerry Hall (Shah of Persia, Mick Jagger). Such a state of affairs cannot have happened accidentally. Mr Ferry might have been better off putting his keen analytical mind to work on the question of why this was so rather than on writing a whingeing and uncommercial dirge about it.

A highly educated man of exceptional talent, Bryan Ferry − admittedly at the height of his powers more than ten years ago − was compared to both Donne and Wordsworth by the heavy-breathers and light-readers of the music press. After fifteen years of wearing the new girl in town as though she was a particularly ornate cufflink or cummerbund, he throws up his hands in horror at what has happened to him. The reason for it is simple: he was in the company of these girls for one reason and one reason only − no, not *that*. Even more than to sleep with them, he was in their company to flaunt them, to *show them off*. Every time he turned up at a première and smiled into the white light of the flashbulbs with a new model on his arm, he was in essence saying 'CORRR! LOOK WHAT I'VE GOT, LADS!' In so many words.

Ferry didn't have to do anything so vulgar as sell his story to the tabloids; every paparazzi picture told the story, the upmarket dirty joke in which the Girl was inevitably the punchline that he wanted the world to hear. For a man of such wealth and talent, it was *his* commercial exploitation of his sex life that was truly pitiable and tacky. Because he had *no need*. To steal because you need to is much less blameworthy than to steal because something flashy catches your eye.

Kiss-and-sell girls are by their very natures mostly unemployable. Lured away early by the glittering promise of glamour by association, they are educated to a minimal degree and fit for very little. The occasional very pretty, very young, very sassy smartie such as Mandy Smith may rise from the ashes of an affair with a career to attend to. But be serious. What are Pierette Le Pen, Jessica Hahn, Fawn Hall, Donna Rice, Angie Bowie and Fiona Wright supposed to do with the rest of their lives? It has been said (by Shelley Winters) that a pretty face is a passport. But it's not – it's a visa, and it runs out fast. There is always a girl a year younger, an inch taller, a pound lighter coming up on the inside rail and making eyes at your meal-ticket. The professional life of a kiss-and-sell girl is marginally shorter than that of a professional tennis player.

There is a slight demographical change in the kiss-and-sell trade on the horizon. For a start, toyboys are starting to sell their stories and any profession which men go into tends to gain status. Men like the members of Duran Duran have started to marry their models, and in tabloid as in law court, wives rarely testify against their husbands.

And there is a certain cachet in *not* telling, started by Kathleen Stark who has emerged from the Duke of York romp with a good deal of the mystery and elegance of an F. Scott Fitzgerald heroine. He actually had a short called 'The Girl The Prince Liked', as good a title as any for the Koo Stark Story.

In the meantime, like abortion, other women may not approve of it for themselves, but any woman worth her salt should defend the right of others to practise it; because to do otherwise is to connive with men in the most craven of ways. Men make the rules, bent as they are, and we should twist them even more for all we are worth. And a man who chooses to go out with a girl he uses only as a human bauble on the glittering boughs of his success, there only to be flaunted and boasted, deserves all he gets when the inanimate object is brought to life by the thunderbolt of malice, turning the tables and exploiting *him*, whether a pop star or a captain of industry.

That's her prerogative. It's a dirty business and she didn't make the rules. Rich and powerful men are not the Untouchables of our society, not an underprivileged minority deserving of protection. If they don't want to wake up and find their foibles on the front page, they should think twice before squiring women with no other means of making a living. In the meantime, they are perfectly allowed to have their crumpet and eat it. But if the crumbs end up as banner headlines, they should desist from bellyaching. And take their medicine like the big men they like to think they are.

DESIGNER DYKES

• • • • • • • •

Blakes Hotel, South Kensington, that black basement which *reeks* of the Seventies version of Twenties decadence, 10.30 Friday night. Over dinner I become aware of the girls at the next table. Pretty, long-haired, well-dressed (who are you calling Alaia?), at first I'd taken them for sisters. But as the Napa Valley Pinot Noir goes into action, they begin to act distinctly . . . oddly. There is a lot of hand-holding, first under the table, then on top of it. 'I do love you, really . . . but it's so complicated.' Tears start to flow as freely as the wine and, around midnight, the dining room breathes a half-relieved, half-disappointed sigh as they cough up and stagger out into the night city holding each other tight as tourniquets. *That's* Designer Dykes.

In the personal column there's an ad: 'GIRL. Come around the world with me. I am a rich and beautiful lesbian looking for a young and pretty girlfriend. NO BUTCHES, LEFTIES OR CRAZIES.' *That's* a Designer Dyke.

In Rome, there is a titled nineteen-year-old from a famous British family, the young women of which are notorious for their beauty and charm, tending to become actresses, marry young and have lots of babies. Not *this* cousin. By day a model, by night she dresses in leather from head to toe and zooms around the Eternal City picking up and dropping the innocent local girls so quick they don't know what hit them (usually her, with her leather motorcycle belt). They say she'll be dead by twenty-one, shot by some enraged paternal peasant. *That's* a Designer Dyke and a half.

A Designer Dyke isn't just any old muff-diver; oh goshi, no. To be in with the invert crowd you must be beautiful, powerful, rich or famous. Having all four won't hurt you. Girl-talking, Queer Street used to be somewhere ideologically right-on and aesthetically depressing, probably in Camden (Peter York had a great line on a certain sort of girl who was around a lot at the start of the Eighties – 'She's a Camden Town, monkey-booted, Julie Covington dyke!') Now it's just as likely to be Beauchamp Place. Stylish lesbianism, full-time, part-time or just plain good-time, is making a comeback. They're even making films about it again: *The Color Purple, Desert Hearts, Mona Lisa, The Berlin Affair*. And the first soap lesbians raised their expensively tousled heads in 1986 – Ciji and Laura of *Knot's Landing*. Even if Ciji did die for her sins. Dykes are bucks, and the shock of the frock troops are the DDs, the smartest ones of all.

There are a few eternals when it comes to men and sex. One, they all like high heels. Two, they all like the idea of two girls doing it to each other. Somewhere in Hampstead, there might even lurk one enlightened man who really doesn't go for heels. But nowhere in the American-speaking world is there a man who would say no to a little dyke action.

And this is no new thing; girls who were young in the Fifties report that 'the first thing a man always wanted you to do after you'd slept with him was do it with another girl, with him in the bed. If you asked them if they'd sleep with another man while you watched, they'd be very shocked and say, ''But it's different for girls! You're so beautiful! It's different!'' . . .' They're still saying it. An anthropologist might call it stepping down in the dominance hierarchy. A feminist might call it male masochism. I'd call it dead pervy. Whatever, the taste is there. It's behind female mud-wrestling, a good deal of soft porn and the noble thespian lesbian tradition of the celluloid catfight, from early James Bond films to late Duran Duran videos. Little Richard admits, 'The first thing I wanted when I got to a new town on tour was two girls who'd go together, because I always found that the most beautiful thing of all.' At the height of his weight and impotence, Elvis could only do the dirty deed after copious viewing of his latest flame with another dame – his wild card up the sleeve was an unbelievably beautiful, unimpeachably skilled Las Vegas lesbian showgirl, who would be flown in on a private plane and guaranteed to have the stainless panties off the purest, most God-fearing Virginia virgin in record time. (Talk about hitting below the Bible-belt.)

But as with most types of titillation – jailbait, force fantasies – hold this one a beat too long and it casts a big shadow. Men have always felt essentially ambivalent about female homosexuality; both thrilled and threatened. They like it when they're the ringmasters and you're prancing like ponies under the whip, when what you're doing is very obviously a substitute for the Real Thing. But held a beat too long, a three in a bed romp becomes an eternal triangle. Many is the enlightened man who goes for the throat when Miss Right gets a bit too fond of Miss X. Doug Lucie wrote a whole play about it, ironically called *Progress*; Lenny Bruce wrote a whole routine about it, ironically called humour, after his wife went along with his wishes once too often. 'Forget the fags – they can't hurt you, no. It's the dykes that'll get you every time. See, you can *recognize* the fags. But you can't recognize the dykes. You know why? Because you're married to them.'

A good number of Eighties DDs were Seventies swingers who first indulged just to keep the boyfriend happy, when he got jaded as Seventies boyfriends were wont to do, and discovered that it could be much more than just another pesky fetish. Conveniently, lesbians are the only group not yet hit by AIDS.

And it's another sort of safe sex. Give or take a tennis palimony or two, famous lesbians do not risk death by tabloid like their male counterparts. This is because, thanks to an essential difference in taste, lesbians are not greatly attracted to the young and the rough, and feel no pressing need to cruise the talkative tenderloin picking up those stool pigeons in rent boy's clothing. Lesbians like sophistication and sleekness, and this means there is no call of the wild forever hanging over their heads like a dildo of Damocles. The feted ones find it easy to keep within an ajar if not closed circle, embracing modelling, the media, the arts, sports and minor royalty. There is a casting couch, but a much smaller one than those the male homosexuals and heterosexuals avail themselves of. Actually, it's more of a love-seat; a bit of handholding and necking, but very little horizontal hanky-panky.

Some people mutter about the Muffia, a network of media women who endlessly lunch, lay and launch each other up the ladder of success, but they're usually the types who believe that God was a Freemason.

Occasionally, though, you might catch the elusive butterfly out of the corner of your eye lunching at Little's, or Tang, or the Sanctuary. The lesbian litmus test? Easy, they'll be eating *fish* . . .

Some are born dykes (the ugly ones), some are made dykes (the clever ones) and some become dykes when men thrust themselves upon them once too often (the pretty ones). Lesbianism is highly *logical*, apart from anything else – much more so than male inversion. Aesthetically, the beauty of women is celebrated in our culture to an extent that the Kamen frères can only dream of; from the time an adolescent girl starts reading the junior glossies at the age of twelve, she is bombarded with barely clothed images of female lusciousness at a time when her male contemporaries are at their most uniquely unattractive. Twelve-year-old girls are natural lesbians, and the boys they choose as Beards – from David Cassidy to Terence Trent D'Arby – reflect this with their pubescent prettiness. They don't look like stinky boys, but like your sweetest-smelling, smoothest girlfriend. (I once knew a rather sheltered twelve-year-old who wondered aloud whether Donny Osmond had started his periods yet.) Show me an adolescent girl who likes Sylvester Stallone, and I'll show you a forty-year-old midget.

Politically, there is no doubt that, as Dick Gregory said, women have been the niggers of the world since the first rape – easily as big a milestone in human history as the first weapon or the first wheel. Just as one can understand blacks who refuse to sleep with whites, one can understand the oppressed sex refusing to collaborate with the oppressor. A white who refuses on principle to sleep with blacks, on the other hand, must be a little morally dubious, just like male homosexuals. You weren't *wronged* by the other side; you just don't *like* them.

But these reasons have been with us for a long time; why now? Small things that add up to a big deal. This generation of DDs were cutting their sexual teeth to a soundtrack of non-stop David Bowie and a cast of thousands of ambisexuals, bisexuals and trisexuals. They started reading the posh Sundays at a time when the first generation of bitter, aborted, sexually-diseased Sixties feminists had discovered 'female friendship' and were banging on about it all over the place. They reached the age of consent with the first crop of warnings about Pill thrombosis and cervical cancer; it seemed a very big price to pay for the pleasure of faking orgasms (another Seventies exposé, when it turned out that the only Big O you could count on was Roy Orbison). *Then* came working out; it sounds silly, but more lesbian affairs have been started in the gym than in a hundred gay bars. Male homosexuals have known this for years; things happen after a communal bath . . .

We have much to thank the Designer Dyke for; she is the antithesis of the boots and braces butch, who was as traitorous a travesty as Danny La Rue or Al Jolson. (Think of Phranc, and what box-office BO *she* turned out to be.) But in rejecting this stereotype, we should not rush to embrace another. Many victims of men turn to girls thinking they'll be 'nicer'. You might get lucky, but you'd be a fool to take it for granted. Gentle readers may not have heard of the 'S & M Dykes' a group of broads who are wont to get together once a week and bash the living daylights out of each other as adeptly as any — boo, hiss — man. Like Jill Johnston, the alleged Seventies feminist who made a point out of sexually harassing waitresses and patronizing strip shows, women can be louses, Lotharios and even Lads.

'Most women are such hypocrites,' says one DD. 'They say "Oh, women are so much nicer than men! I love them every way, except sexually." Garbage! I've only got *time* for them sexually! As people, 90 per cent of them are vain, pretentious and completely incapable of telling the truth. As a friend, give me a man every time. Men are so much more *decent*.' Another Filofox says, 'I gave up girls because I missed the adoration I got from men. It wasn't until I tried lesbianism that I realized what men, the poor bastards, have to go through before they can get their end away. Girls, especially the pretty ones, are too used to being adored and reassured; you don't know what boredom is until you spend all evening listening to some bimbo talk about herself exclusively – her face, her body, her diet, her career. Just think, men go through it all the time. I thought it would be less so, but there was *more* of a power struggle than there is with men. Men are strong enough to be soft. Women have just got too uppity.'

Queer Street – take a walk on the wild side *and* keep your figure. The blend of health-consciousness and depravity is singularly suited to this jaded yet scared decade. In the Eighties, lesbianism is about the one pleasurable activity you can indulge in that won't make you fat or sick. To paraphrase the Milky Way ad, it's the one thing you can eat without spoiling your appetite – or your cervix.

But nothing is as simple as it seems, especially faith healing. Girls won't rape you or get you pregnant. They won't give you thrombosis or cancer or AIDS. They probably won't forget your birthday or be unsympathetic when you have the cramps. But they might bore you, and they might just break your heart.

Seminal DDs

- Dolly Wilde (some relation)
- Christabel Pankhurst and Eva Gore-Booth
- Radclyffe Hall and Una, Lady Troubridge
- Vita Sackville-West
- Lakey Eastlake in *The Group* (blue-blooded, blue-stocking DD)
- Vivien Taube (in the expurgated bit of *Tender is the Night*)
- Hollywood aristocracy DDs: Janet Gaynor, Claudette Colbert, Natacha Rambova, Dietrich, Garbo, Bankhead (at wedding of two friends: 'I've had them both, and they were both awful')
- Anita Pallenberg (in *Barbarella* 'Come to me, my pretty pretty')
- Stephane Audran and Jacqueline Sassard (in *Les Biches*)
- Jean Seberg (in *Lilith* – DD goes gaga)
- Gertrude Stein
- Martina Navratilova (a quintessential DD for her impeccable wealth, her Born Again capitalism and complete purging of any political content from her sexual preference)
- Maria Schneider (for bravery and beauty beyond the call of duty. First and only trendy Seventies bisexual sex symbol to break for the border and declare UDI – Unequivocal Dyke Independence – pretty much ruining her career in the process)

BEAUTY AND THE BEASTS

· · · · · · · ·

Eric Morley, creator of the Miss World contest, is not the sort of man you would want to meet on a crowded, well-lit street. He looks like Reg Varney and behaves like Napoleon; his hair looks like an oil slick and with his wife Julia – who looks like a bathing beauty who went to work at Broadmoor – they became in the early Seventies the Juan and Evita Peron of the British leisure industry. With their birds and bingo between them, they had the proletariat bowing towards Mecca more surely than any Islamic imam. But pride comes before a fall and in 1979 came the payoff; Morley was dismissed from Mecca. The wide boy who would be a Tory MP had fallen; it was the end of an era.

They say that behind every great man is a great woman; filling in for her, meanwhile, was Julia. Half monster, half matron, she was the Mommie Dearest to generations of young women born to sleep with George Best. She never stopped standing by her man – give or take a few brief shining moments taking tea and tango with her dashing Argentinian just-good-friend. There is something, barely contained, big and brassy about her; you can see her in your mind's eye on the wrong side of midnight at the

Morley mansion, the mascara slightly smeared, singing along to Shirley Bassey's bloody but unbowed mega-ballad 'This Is My Life'.

The Morleys' baby, Miss World, is thirty-five this year. Just like the Eurovision Song Contest, it is one of those annual pieces of processed entertainment, both hackneyed and amateurish, which everyone loathes and yet loves to watch. It has always been tempting to see such beauty contests as *Stepford Wives* in bathing suits, the terminal feminist nightmare, but the fact is that beauty contests have very little to do with the ideal of women as sex objects. What is on display is an archaic icon of chastity and femininity; Miss World, or Miss Smalltown, is a creature of grooming and deportment much more than bosoms and behinds – an ideal of Lucie Clayton, not Bob Guccione. She is what local heroines with big dreams and little else do when they want to go places other than straight from the youth club to the antenatal clinic. This is perhaps the greatest deception of all: the winners are promised the world – they end up opening supermarkets in Weston-super-Mare before embarking on a life as the second wife of a used-car salesman.

In thirty-five years, Miss World, the biggest competition of its kind, has produced from the cornucopian horn of career opportunities a handful of bit parts in Bond films – Carolyn Seaward, Mary Stavins – a marriage to Bruce Forsyth – Wilnelia Merced – and a baby by Bob Marley – Cindy Breakspeare. The girls go through a year of living out of suitcases and signing autographs before handing over the crown and retiring into affluent, anonymous private lives. There is always some provincial businessman big in software who would love nothing better than to boast that his Mrs was once Miss World, so one thing these girls are never lacking in is potential husbands, even if they are not of the calibre of the international crooner who briefly serenades them on the stage of the Albert Hall. If they give interviews five years after being demobbed, they invariably display disappointment and bafflement about the prize and the promises and the paucity of real opportunity the title awarded them. Rather like winning the Eurovision Song Contest, winning Miss World is often hazardous to the health of your career.

One reason why beauty contests tend not to produce world-beaters could be because, like the Eurovision itself, acts of real calibre will not enter it. Real beauty or real talent is inherently aligned to great ego, and very unwilling to parade itself like a prize poodle for the less than Olympian judgement of one brain-damaged boxer, one overweeningly preening male hairdresser, one permed footballer and one sneering thirty-five-year-old starlet, of which the Miss World panels are generally composed. There are no big beauties in these contests, especially the domestic ones – despite being the allegedly most beautiful girls in the country, you never see beings who look like Lesley Anne Down or Sade Adu in the Miss Great Britain bash.

The girls are judged on malleability much more than mammaries – hence the painfully brief and banal 'chat' with the smarmy Radio Two DJ (for Dumb Jerk) or the Breakfast TV gamine from which their 'personalities' are miraculously supposed to emerge in the space of thirty seconds. And if beauty is in the eye of the beholder, perhaps next year's Miss GB should be renamed Miss GBH and transmitted in Braille. Some of the contestants are ugly enough to frighten small children; some are pretty, impeccably slender, tanned to a creamy golden sheen and perfectly symmetrical – but then so is a packet of processed cheese slices. One thing is sure: beauty never raises its unsettling head. Beauty can be an awe-inspiring and even frightening thing; you never feel awe watching a beauty contest though you sometimes feel awful. Watching the Miss Great Britain beauty contest, you see moderately attractive Anglo-Saxon girls who might, if they're lucky, get a part as a mute receptionist in *Crossroads*. Beauty contests should be renamed pretty contests.

This is the West, where being a beauty contestant is something of the distaff-and-diaphragm version of being a boxer – something you wouldn't really choose to do if you had a chance of succeeding at something else. In the West, real beauties go straight into showbusiness, where the reward, in cents and celebrity both, is so great. They become singers, or actresses, or fashion and photographic models. In the American-speaking world – the USA, Europe West and Australasia – the modelling business is so above-board and legitimately lucrative that girls from extremely prominent families choose to stoop to conquer it. Christie Brinkley's father is a millionaire TV executive; Rachel Ward, who started as a model, is the daughter of Lady Penelope Dudley Ward; the great English models of the Sixties, Shrimpton and Mallett and Hammond, were all fastidiously-reared upper-middle Home Counties gels, swinging Sloanes, which is why Twiggy was such a well-publicized and gimmicky hit – it was her drunken parrot Neasden squawk as much as her swimming-pool eyes.

In the Third World countries modelling and other professional means of making the monetary most of beauty are synonymous with prostitution – it was only in the last century that 'actress' meant prostitute in Britain, hence the bishop and the actress jokes – and beauty contests such as the heavily-chaperoned, censorious Miss World are one way in which girls can draw attention to their looks without ruining their marriage prospects. The Latin American girls who have been favourites in the Eighties – a few years ago, Julia Morley created a controversy of her own when she admitted that because of the small scandals surrounding British, American and West German winners in the Seventies, there was now an unofficial bias towards Latin American girls because 'character' (meaning in Morleyspeak a complete absence of same, and utter malleability) was now being taken into consideration when picking winners – tend to be very young students from middle-class families, religious and used to being bossed around by their elders. Mrs Morley can tell a Latin girl when to sleep, eat and smile for the camera, and the girl will not turn a tinted hair; tell a Northern girl to go to bed – alone – at ten, and she'll tell you where to stick your Miss World sceptre.

This variance in attitude, together with the fact that Third World beauty has not been creamed off into showbusiness proper as it has in the West, has queered the pitch for Western contestants in recent years. Though the current winner comes from Finland, it is no coincidence that her country is far from the madding crowd and dull as ditchwater, and her profession the impossibly worthy one of primary school teacher. A certain pattern is being soundly stuck to, morally if not geographically.

The silliness of the Miss World spectacle occasionally

clashes incongruously with the wretched real lives of its Third World contestants. In the Sixties, Maita Gomez was a runner-up representing the Philippines. Less than twenty-four hours later, she was in the Filipino jungle fighting the murderous regime of Ferdinand Marcos with the country's Communist guerillas. In the Seventies, Miss El Salvador sought political sanctuary in Canada, claiming that she was on the death list of a Right-wing terrorist group in her own country. In the excitable and shallow days of the early Seventies, some misguided souls thought that teetering down a catwalk of your own free will wearing stilettoes, a swimsuit and a smile was a political issue in itself. In 1970, a hundred women in evening dress infiltrated the audience at the Albert Hall where Bob Hope was compering the Miss World contest; at a signal they ran down the aisles casting plastic mice and leaflets into the crowd and throwing stink bombs, smoke bombs and bags of flour at the stage. It might have been wiser to distribute these party treats in reverse, considering that the girls were probably more intelligent than the audience and would have stood a better chance of making sense of the leaflets while the audience, as with boxing matches, was vastly more objectionable than the competitors and much more deserving of a plague of Homepride.

Afterwards they said they had been protesting against the 'narrow destiny of women', and wrote in a pamphlet assessing the event, 'We've been in the Miss World contest all our lives . . . judging ourselves as the judges judge us.' And indeed, the most pathetic part of a beauty contest is when the winner, wobbling down the flimsy golden pathway, weeps, not with happiness, but with *relief* – because the self-important flotsam and jetsam, the dregs of the celebrity circus who make up the panel, have found her *not lacking*. Trial by trash.

The beauty queen's tears are a good barometer of women's quite pathological dependence on the approval of others, the dependence that stops them from doing so much. But this is just a symptom, not the sickness. Beauty contests on the whole are *not* sexist – not like the serious issues such as discrimination and violence – but simply pulchritudist. And pulchritudinism is a vice found as often in women as in men – or else the actors and singers that young and old women worship, from Paul Newman to Jason Donovan, would not so invariably be pretty faces first and foremost.

Feminism and its capricious demands has even filtered through to the sublimely stupid talking heads who interview the girls, albeit fifteen years after the event, and now some poor young thing is invariably and brutally told, 'You know, some people think contests like these are degrading. What do you say to that?' One often wishes the girls would lash out with their Cutex claws and cite the textbook feminists' banquet of body hair and dearth of D-cup as a reason for their rhetoric, but they are so well-drilled and passively feminine that they dare not even defend themselves in case it is seen as aggression. 'It's a matter of opinion,' they chirp. 'Everyone's entitled to their own beliefs.' I remember a Miss United Kingdom contestant some years ago who actually went too far and said thoughtfully, 'Yes, I see their point.' She didn't win.

The days have gone when beauty contests caused anger; now they fire no more exciting grist for the front page than boredom, condescension and very mild contempt. Beauty contestants have been left to their own

71

devices, and other, dumber animals have attracted the chivalrous attentions of the boys and girls in balaclavas. The only protest the Miss World contest has seen in recent years was a scuffle by animal rights protestors drawing attention to the wanton wearing of fur coats, which the girls had been doing during some half-baked photographic session which was part of the tepid promotion build-up to the night of a thousand thighs. And the only feminist voices raised against the competition recently have been those protesting that black girls never win, and that the girls are judged by European ethnocentric standards of beauty. Feminists now complain about women *not* winning beauty contests rather than winning them.

Beauty contests are a sucked orange, much too redundant to boil blood. They are just a little Western gimmick, neither here nor there in the endless debit against women's balance in the real world. When one considers what women in other parts of the world have to go through to be considered beautiful – neck stretching, foot binding, genital mutilation – a bit of back-combing is hardly anything worth writing home (or to *Spare Rib*) about.

P. T. Barnum staged the first recorded beauty contest in 1855; the first Miss America contest took place in 1921; Miss World originated in 1951. The beauty contest is a product of the chaste, look-but-don't-touch pre-Sixties world, and no major one has been invented since. They do not correspond with the ideals of modern men or the ambitions of modern women; the Miss World retreat into the feudal virgins of Latin America, the way they dare not give the title to a Westerner (Finland is Europe East, and the girls in Europe East are almost as obedient and down-trodden as the Latins) with a mind and a sex drive of her own reflects the impossible contradictions between Miss World and the modern world. The competition may as well be renamed Miss Olde Worlde.

The only new and growing (swelling, in this case) contests based on physical appearance are the muscle shows, in which men and women alike are judged by how *powerful*, not how passive, they look. These new narcissists are the subjects of films and videos and TV documentaries; the first muscle millionaire (Arnold Schwarzenegger) has been made, and the first female muscle millionaire is only a steroid away. Already they appear on chat shows and model in *Cosmopolitan* – things that beauty queens can only dream of doing, modest as they are.

Last year, America saw the emergence of a new group of pubescent girls – the Wannabes, so-called because whenever a TV reporter came within a twenty-mile radius they would squeal 'We wannabe rich and famous, we wannabe Madonna!' They *didn't* want to be Miss World – it seems so pitifully *little* to ask from life to the growing Wannabe. They want to be Madonna, aggressive, predatory and outrageous, the direct opposite of the Miss World ideal. And as for the girl herself, 'I wanna rule the world,' she says when asked *her* ambition, and you will notice she didn't enter the Miss America contest to achieve it.

The girls who continue to put themselves forward for inspection by washed-up old has-beens hardly qualified to judge any human quality, let alone youth and beauty, seem more mocked, more doomed to their complete powerlessness and anonymity every year as they clutch their fake crowns and sceptres and sit on their fake thrones digesting the fake horizons that are laid open to them by the oily courtiers of the so-called most beautiful girl in the world, the queen of beauty. Do you doubt their waning appeal? A test: in a celebrity-crazed world where even the lowliest starlet's name is household, do *you* know the name of the reigning most beautiful girl in the world?

I'M ONLY HERE FOR THE BEARD

. . . .

> 'Never trust a man with a beard: he's
> trying to hide something'
>
> My Mother

Nikki is a Beard. She's not really Nikki, though 'Nikki' is a suitable pseudonym — accent on the *pseud* — for a Beard. Beards favour names which end in an 'i' or which could be boys' names or both — Shari, Sasha, Stacey. To her social superiors the 'i' sounds very 'me' and thus NQOTD; to the Beard herself it indicates classlessness and disregard for restricting tradition, while the boys' names indicate jolliness, palliness, a girl not waxing or waning with the moon or the womb. It is hard to imagine a girl who calls herself 'Nikki' getting inadvertently pregnant.

The only thing Nikki gets inadvertently is jet-lag. Nikki is a Show Business Beard. What is a Show Business Beard? To put things plainly (very UnBeard — they don't like giving anything its real name, especially what they do) Beards are girls who pretend to be sleeping with homosexual celebrities so that said celebrities are not revealed as homosexual. Beards are as essential a part

75

of show business as wearing shades after dark and trying suicide on for size.

Beards began with history but really took off in Hollywood – probably with Valentino, who started so many things still put through their paces by pop stars (see Prince's *Under the Cherry Moon*). He married his Beard, Natacha Rambova; like her, the goatee Beards of the Twenties and Thirties were often celebrity lesbians with as much to hide as their better halves – arrangements known as Twilight Tandems or Lavender Liaisons. Sex symbols by their very nature must be narcissistic, and narcissism – the mirror image making love to oneself, like a centipede – is thought to be an important component of homosexuality. The Hollywood Sign, that sad, stage-struck Statue of Liberty, was an avenging angel of an escape route for narcissistic homosexual men, so much so that a Fifties film like *Giant* can feature a hat-trick of homosexuals – Hudson, Dean and Mineo; more fruits than Del Monte, my dear! – in the principal male roles. But when Hollywood lost its glamour it lost its pull: now these boys flocked instead to the new boom-town, which had its (inch-thick) foundations in amoral luck and the fast buck as much as the original.

In the Fifties, when the length of a pop star's eyelashes mattered more than the score of his IQ, every casting couch in Tin Pan Alley had wings for horizontal upward mobility. But with the arrival of the Beatles and the other arrogant, autonomous singer-songwriters, things changed – boys were no longer to be had for the price of a recording contract, and the lecherous Svengali became superfluous; Brian Epstein's goldmine ironically made him a man out of time. The minds behind the behinds became revered, and the pop stars stopped being the game and became the hunters, first tracking down well-bred southern dollybirds – Jane, Patti, Marianne – and then homely, nest-building Aunt Sallies – Yoko, Linda. It was now that the love-lives of pop stars became second only in the speculation stakes to the love-lives of heirs to the throne of the United Kingdom. Everyone had an opinion, usually the same one – 'Why didn't he marry that nice Jane Asher?' was as often a repeated early Seventies English homily as 'The unions are holding the country to ransom' and 'What's that in real money?'

The Seventies saw the rise of the Ligmalions – girls like Angie, Jerry, Britt, Bianca – who, bored with lower-middle class life in dull towns in Scandinavia or Latin America or Texas had *re-invented* themselves just like the good fairy Helen Gurley Brown had promised, part of the process being to date a pop star. These girls were all associated with men whose images were *sexually flexible*, to say the least, and it was the effeminacy of their mincing meal-tickets which made these charismatic vacuums seem much stronger than they really were.

This year's model is altogether different. To some extent the Seventies girls buried the men they set out to praise and raise with their presence – in some cases they made them appear ridiculous (Britt Ekland dressing up the Lad icon Rod Stewart in top-hat and tails; she might as well have pinned a *bunny*tail on him, considering the laughing-stock she made of him), and in most the pairings coincided with a drastic loss of cred and record sales and numerous accusations of jetsam-set sell-out.

Things had to change. The Beards went out and the Birds came back. The much-photographed marriages of Duran Duran to a giggle of models and dancers – what with the Danish girlfriend Renee, the Anglo-Iranian Yasmin, the Jewish-American Julianne, the Italian Giovanna and the English Tracey, they at one point resembled a UN of flash flesh – reflected the new pattern of chosen consort: a pretty glamour-profession nobody with her own money. Pop stars tend not to marry famous – or notorious – girls any more; it makes you look henpecked and hijacked. *No one* wants to be Rod Stewart, made to appear a mere bauble by the blondes he sought to wear like cufflinks.

Sex is all about the birds and the Beards when you're a household face. Birds are the conspicuously consumed crumpet carried on arms to nightclubs by pop stars rampant, trying to keep up with the Tom Joneses. The Beard, on the other hand, is a boy's best friend and nothing more; his confidante and cover for a love that these days dare not sing its name. She is the sexual triumph of form over content. And she's more in demand now than she's ever been. Boy George – before the Troubles – was pop homosexuality's cuddly last gasp. Then came AIDS. With the birth of the first British HTLV3-positive baby in January 1986, gender-bending's fate was sealed – modern young parents who might once have bought their offspring the product of a man in a frock with an indulgent chuckle are now more likely to be burning said product on manicured back lawns, supposing they allow it in the house in the first place. The careers of the Ladyshave Wave – Marilyn, George, Peter Burns – as opposed to their trials and tribulations, are conspicuous by their absence. (N.B. Boy George may now have a conspicuous teenage girlfriend, Alice Temple, but rumours of his reform are greatly exaggerated.)

In the Seventies crooners could be glad to be gay. Elton John, David Bowie and Tom Robinson all came out, and the empresses' new clothing was much admired; being bisexual was as fashionable as being bilingual. There was a famous photograph of Bowie, Jagger and Lou Reed having a cuddle in a nightclub – they might as well have been having a cocktail for all the eyelids that were batted. Tom Robinson could sing 'Glad To Be Gay' without provoking a mass stampede for the exit: try it now. You might as well shout 'FIRE!' in a crowded auditorium or 'AIDS!' during an orgy. Being gay, in the collective consciousness, is no longer daring but dangerous.

Enter the drag-on: the Beard. She is the minder of the gay pop star's masculinity, keeping gossips at bay with her beauty. She does not wish to convert the glittering prize but comfort him in comfort, preferably in the West Indies. Between them, AIDS and the new pop focus of the gossip columns have brought the Beard back with a bang – or at least with a photogenic French kiss in the VIP lounge and a discreetly held hand on the table at the BPI Awards. Luckily, the Beard tends not to be too interested in sex for its own sake – she thinks fellatio is an opera by Mozart.

The Beard is back in more than one style. There is the Detachable Beard – the one who goes out with more than one pop star. There is the Five O'Clock Shadow – the Beard with the crop. There is the Transatlantic Beard – the 'girlfriend in America' some young household faces refer to vaguely. There are Beard jokes: 'What's it like kissing a man with a Beard?', 'Fine, as long as he sends her out of the room first.' Then there is Nikki, a real girl, a real Beard. Nikki, isn't it a little . . . deceitful? 'NO! A lot of show business is . . . *pretend*. Most people's hair colour comes out of a bottle . . . is that *deceit*? It's just *show business.*'

And the show must go on. So Nikki wends her weary beat from South Molton Street to North Africa; she might have left school with one Art O-level but she knows a lot that other girls of twenty-three don't, especially about airports. She spends more time in them than your average cracked jumbo jet, always being snapped sharing a joke (too right) on the way back from Montserrat or Ocho Rios. Nikki doesn't get colds or PMT, she gets jet-lag. She calls it the Curse.

This is why Beards never kiss and tell (with the exception of one with a rich fantasy life who occasionally, with the nod from his manager, sells stories of her nights of love with a rampantly camp crooner). It's an extremely cushy life. Tell a paper and you get a lousy five-figure sum and then you have to get a job – and the Star Bar is suddenly off limits. Don't tell and you might get to be the Beard of three household faces before you've lost your puppy fat. Keep a clean nose and a wide eye and a buttoned lip and there's even a chance your wearer may marry you; it has been known. One famous Seventies pop star married his Beard and complained nine months later that they were having problems spawning. 'Does he know he has to fuck her first?' Nikki asked me in a rare moment of bad temper.

Most boys don't marry their Beards, though – always a Beard, never a bride. By their waistlines they live and by their waistlines they perish. An old Beard is a sad sight, and they can be old at twenty-six: a shell of a girl cut adrift with no skills or purpose. Funny, they come around the schools warning you about the addictive, detrimental powers of drink and drugs and early sex, but

they don't tell you about the biggest, baddest soul-
destroyer of all: the addictive, detrimental power of
reflected glory, glory not paid for with adolescent isolation
and adult grind.

This is the way things are. Next time you stand in the
rain waiting for a bus and you see a picture in the paper
of Her, bronzed and blasé at some airport, send up a
prayer for the girl on the arm of the golden boy; for she
too will know sorrow.

SEX ZOMBIES

. . . .

She sang sometimes in a club or at a private party. Not very well: it was herself she so cleverly produced and marketed; herself that other people needed so much she did not have to do more than be there on offer. Her effaced obliterated quality, her frightened sexuality, a brave passivity, was so much to a current taste that she was known to 'everyone'. She was in fact a type of courtesan. Many gentlemen prepared to pay highly for their pleasures paid to accompany her to parties, to be seen publicly with this girl who was The Victim incarnate. She might even sleep with them, but without any pretence of enjoyment. Her attitude was: If you enjoy what so wearies me then please . . . I should be delighted. Sex was not the essence of what they offered or what was wanted from them. Girls like Zena were prized for their *style*, a highly-dramatized and self-conscious 'I am a lost soul' quality. They drifted listlessly, displaying their psychological wounds like medals, or as if saying, 'This is what you have made of me. But I bear you no grudge. Please hit me again!'

Doris Lessing, *The Four-Gated City*, 1969

I walked with a sex zombie, sometime in 1985. She was nineteen and came from Woking. She took lots of cocaine and heroin. She was lousy with A-levels but embarrassed, concealing them the way old-fashioned girls would abortions. Arabs loved her; you could see why. She was very blonde and frigid. And she was very sweet. You could tell she didn't have orgasms because when you dished up some particularly luscious dessert she'd close her eyes and moan 'Ohhh. Orgasm.' (I've never been able to confuse Marks & Spencer Individual Lemon Cheesecake with the Big O, myself. Sara Lee Blackcurrant, that's a different matter.) She had scars. She got hit. She read Proust, pouting – she put the pout into PrOUsT. (Odette was a Sex Zombie.) In the end she reluctantly let go of our mutual friend, sick of love and poverty and the damage they both did you, her fingers uncurling slowly like those of a drowning man in a dream. The next time I saw her was on the cover of a magazine, faking laughter, looking like a Marilyn.

When I finally called, her agent said she'd just got out of hospital. You knew why. Starlets don't get sick, they have O.D.s and operations. She answered the phone with a strangulated little howl, 'Yaaas?'

'Sara,' (I'll call her Sara because that's her name) 'are you all right?'

'Well, darling, I've just come out of hospital . . .'

'Abortion or overdose?'

'How did you guess? Yah, I had an abortion and it went wrong and . . . yeurgh . . .'

Looking like a Marilyn, living like a Marilyn. That night she turned up in the swank SW7 basement where she used to work as a waitress, in a dress as tight as a tourniquet and as black as a bruise. Strong women wept into their vichyssoise. She looked like a million dollars and had £5.50 in the bank. That night London belonged to her as I pushed her through its extortionate doorways, taking care to follow five steps behind like an Arab wife.

Starlet starlet on the screen/Who will follow Norma Jean? Ever since her death by deification in the Sixties, legions of sumptuously sad, semi-sensitive, non-specific girls have used her as an alternative convent. The adoption of her hair colour takes the place of the shave and the wimple; not brides of Christ, but brides of Marilyn, their spiritual core not penetrable by man. They go from casting couch to shrinking couch, taking care to drink heavily, O.D. copiously and abort religiously along the way. Hundreds become household (or at least locker-room) names, but thousands don't.

Sara probably will; she has the same stifled intelligence, the same bitchy sweetness, the same obliterated quality, frightened sexuality and brave passivity of both Mailer's Marilyn and Lessing's Zena. Since then her legs have been in the *Face*, her face has been in *ID* and her shamelessness all over the Street of Shame's fashion spreads. Like Marilyn, whose angel-food prettiness never came near the blood-curdling beauty of Elizabeth Taylor circa *Cat On A Hot Tin Roof* or Ava Gardner in the Forties ('The most beautiful woman in the world,' said Elizabeth Taylor of Gardner; 'She's got everything, I've got nothing,' said Monroe of Taylor), Sara is not the prettiest or most sexually arousing girl in the world. But that obliterated quality is hot, hot, hot right now – Sex Zombie Chic, Le Style Somnambuliste, which found its original glowing persona in poor moribund Marilyn, a girl so dislocated and disconnected from life that she even seemed to be *breathing* through gauze, like a baby in an incubator.

'I don't know what the fuss was all about; she was the worst sort of person, totally helpless,' sniffed Miss Victoria Principal of the dead saint. *O tempora mores!* O victorious principle! O mean, lean and leotarded self-sculpted gold-digger turned born-again Seventies go-go-for-it girl! *You* may not know, but the little Eighties girls understand.

Sex Zombie Chic in your high street is Kim Basinger, a good actress for a good ten years but only just now a name. In the Seventies and early Eighties she was stuck in telefilms and mini-series; exploited in *Portrait Of A Centerfold*, prostituted in *From Here To Eternity*, and incredibly, cast as a self-assertive policewoman in *Cat And Dog* (it didn't make the Neilsens, natch). But come the hour, come the houri. It took the late Eighties to prove that a pretty girl is like a malady and to find Miss Basinger imperilled in *Never Say Never Again*, handcuffed in *No Mercy*, beaten in *Fool For Love* and blindfolded in *9½ Weeks*. Later, much later, she claimed in the *Mail On Sunday* that she had been 'humiliated' by the film, but did it anyway. *Very* Zena – 'But I bear you no grudge. Please hit me again!'

Directors did, and now she is a Film Star while the infinitely more beautiful and sexy contenders, those empirical English brunettes like Lesley-Anne Down, Rachel Ward and Amanda Pays who got such a good headstrong start in films in the Seventies and early Eighties have been retired prematurely to the same mini-series that Basinger has just scraped off her Blahniks.

Basinger is Battered Blonde incarnate, as Marilyn (it

seems brutal to refer to her by her surname, like a thick-skinned public schoolboy) was Baby Blonde, Kelly was Bitch Blonde and West was Hard-Boiled Blonde. Basinger has the vulnerability, class and intelligence of each and – here starteth the lesson – a fat lot of good it does her. A fat lot of *lip* it gets her.

Before the bitches got free, He-man you-man could make do with Marilyn, who merely held the spongey promise of maximum bruisability. Now the bitches are bringing two out of every three divorces, because they're *bored* as often as not (whereas before they clung to man and marriage through beatings, bad breath and mass adultery with the Bluebell Troupe), you need Basinger's throwback manifesto of a face. Her eyes *wince*, her lips are swollen, her face is puffy – if *Oui* ran a Battered Model's Refuge, she would be its personification. Her face is the proof of the pounding.

Why now? She's been coming round that mountain that groans under the burden of dreams of the Hollywood sign for a long time; through Cathy Moriarty in *Raging Bull*, Maud Addams in *Tattoo*, Michelle Pfeiffer in *Scarface*, Nastassja Kinski in *Paris*, *Texas* (tellingly blonde; gentlemen prefer blondes because they're better backdrops for the bruises), Irina Brook in *Captive* and Isabella Rossellini in *Blue Velvet*. Of course you can trace it all the way, like a wavy welt down a long white back, through *Belle de Jour* to *Pandora's Box*. Somebody up there – the front office – has decreed that women want rape, incest, prostitution, degradation and death.

Occasionally, of course, they do. But men, as any prostitute worth the salt she rubs into the lucrative wounds will tell you, want it much, much more. The incidence of male masochism to female masochism is overwhelming; yet it never, strangely, finds its way on to the popular screen. You've got your *Maitresse*, which is arty, or your *Personal Services*, which is farcey – but you never see male masochism as high-fashion soft-focus fashion-accessory. And you wonder why.

There's one main reason: scared men. Men are *very* scared now, as scared as you get without dying of it. Just when you thought it was safe to go back into the singles bar, 88 per cent of American women between eighteen and twenty-eight approve of feminism – *that's* scary. Observing the physical repulsiveness and failed relationships (often with the same actresses they terrorize onscreen) of many modern directors – they all look like Charles Manson, for some reason – one can't help recalling Hitchcock and the bullying lust he used like a weapon against his acute objects of desire, onscreen and off. All these men are dogs, and how much more so when gilded with the adolescent medals of acne; bashing Basinger, they get back at the cheerleader who turned them down in front of their buddies, and the wife who wants the pre-nuptial agreement reassessed. Take that, you bitch! Cut!

Ostensibly a decade of liberation, it was the Sixties which acted as a Sex Zombie *smorgasbord*, when you had even less excuse not to be used. Germaine Greer, a veteran of the Venereal Wars, called the Sixties a time when more joyless liberties were taken with women than any other. And to judge by the indecent haste with which the alternative pushovers of the Sixties became the lesbian separatists, celibates and born-again-virgins of the Seventies, the alternative boys were as bad at providing alternative orgasms as Mr Clean.

The Sixties had a Sex Zombie for every taste: Goldie Hawn was an SZ with laughs, Jean Seberg an SZ with politics. The decade was ruled by Zombie-fanciers: Ward, Warhol, Polanski, Hefner. Ward liked them for their malleability, Warhol for their exploitability, Polanski for their vulnerability (the ultimate Sex Zombie auteur; even a termagant like Lady Macbeth comes out as a slip of a somnambuliste) and Hefner because they could be handed out like poker chips to the unappetizing demi-celebs who flocked to the Bunny Mansions.

Sharon Tate's killing was the Sex Zombie Altamont. But unless they're killed or do themselves in, old Sex Zombies never die; they just get mugged by gravity. Some of the Fifties models married well, having no illusions about eternal youth, but the Sixties lot held it a beat too long and now look well tacky. Rod on Britt: 'I didn't *buy* her book, I stole it at an airport and threw it away when I'd finished. She's so pathetic . . . such a loser. It's always *her* getting dumped, never the other way around.' Men do cheat on SZs a lot and don't really like to marry them. (The sequel to *Gentlemen Prefer Blondes* was called *But They Marry Brunettes*.) Her currency and collateral is all invested in that optimum opportunistic split-second of youth, and she has none of the sexpertise that sees many fascinators well into old age. She loses value easily, and when she gets the young artistic lover instead of the ancient and filthy rich philistine, her days are numbered. She either gets maudlin – Christine Keeler, D and D on the dole, saying 'I regret my life terribly' – or creative – Susan George at thirty-seven producing a slim volume of 'very personal and private' poetry, saying 'Writing is God's gift to me.' Either way, neither's much fun, and a new generation of potential

SZs are making a point of steering clear of it – English safe sex-kittens like Smith and Kensit and Ridley and Fox. Ambitious and rapacious, their patron saint is Madonna and the manifesto which suits their needs and their attention spans her line 'I thought of losing my virginity as a career move' – as far from the Sex Zombie plea 'Do anything you like to me but be nice!' as you can get.

But up there on the big screen, women are mush again. And the more women get their freedom in the mezzanine, the more their onscreen representatives are going to get punished for it. The arty, sophisticated men will keep insisting that it doesn't *mean* anything, that these films *aren't* an upmarket version of 'She asked for it, Your Honour!' A wonderful piece of reporting in last year's *Independent* saw the showing of *Blue Velvet* in Johannesburg as pointing to a new 'era of enlightenment' in the application of South Africa's censorship laws. But isn't it perfectly in line for a sadistic state to show a sadistic film?

And pardon my cheek, but during my own youthful adventures in the wonderful world of S&M, I noticed that black men were much keener on being whipped and otherwise humiliated than women of any colour. Would a film which showed a black man enjoying sexual pain inflicted by a white be as acceptable to a civilized audience, I wonder? Eddie Murphy in the Isabella Rossellini part? Why not?

More women are attacked and killed every day for being women than blacks are for being black. Just *why* is violence against women such a safe, soft artball to play with, and violence against blacks not?

Men. Pity them. Brawn, that bulging ace up the sleeve of man, has never been such a buyers' market. The men who got the sands of Iwo Jima kicked in their faces have won. The new jobs have made sure that muscle is a mark of Cain; a thing of useless beauty or crippling deformity.

The violent criminals rot, five to a cell; the beauty kings pose, oiled like Balinese temple dancers, on the catwalk; the actors bluff on the big screen, desperately winning wars that men of their size and shade and stars and stripes lost years ago to one of the most impeccably delicate armies ever to wear black pyjamas on the job. All of them moribund parodies of the way men used to want to be when they imagined that brute force could get them the girl, the job, the life they wanted – all of them shadow-boxing with extinction.

Man at bay; drunk, punchy, weighed down with the useless blubber that used to pass for penis and power, partly paralysed but trying to make a fist, to HIT BACK, literally below the belt, in the only way they know how. The new sadism of the cinema does not indicate contempt or even a jaded palate, but FEAR, stark, staring, bug-eyed *fear*. The woman who is bound, gagged and beaten is the only woman in the world, it seems to man at bay, who won't get up, walk out and go to work, leaving you to watch the daytime soap operas. So fasten your cinema seatbelts and welcome back the Sex Zombie, because it's going to be a long and bumpy ride.

SENSIBILITY

McLaren's Children

. . . .

It's hard to credit that somewhere in the Nineties, people will welcome the idea of an Eighties revival; no decade in the post-war era has had such a bad press from both highbrows and hip. At least the 'conformist' Fifties had Frankie Sin and the dry martini, the 'messy' Sixties had the mini and the Mods and the 'apocalyptic' Seventies had Biba lipstick and the sound of Philadelphia.

But the Eighties were lost to us, buried beneath the clichés of carping hacks and the duck-billed platitudes of playwrights pissed off that sitting in the mud at festivals went out of style. Its salient images all speak with Biblical portent of moral decline and the worship of Mammon and mammaries; Samantha Fox on the floor of the Big Bang-day Stock Exchange would have been the perfect Eighties photo-opportunity. Greedy City boys, selfish Yuppies, smug Sloanes, post-modern towers of Babylon and inhuman 'isms' by the score: worra life, eh?

But there was another Eighties; a kid with one eye on the mirror and the other on the main chance – status conscious, yes, but bad, uncaring, greedy? Nah – neither a saint nor a sinner, just someone tired of being on the Right-On, street-cred ropes with their nose pressed up against Langan's windowpane, graced with a bit of talent and a lot of front and a desire to move on up.

What made the Eighties culturally unique was that for the first time the dichotomy and division between Hip (marginal; in the know and in the red) and Cube (mainstream; on the make and in the money) finally ended with the two sides falling into each other's armistice. Hip wanted the cash and career that only the Cube could provide; Cube wanted the kudos in return. Anyway, this opposition had always been more of a theological necessity than a reality; there have always been those at the sharp end of Hip who knew that if they didn't move into the mainstream PDQ it would be fifty years of hard labour treading water at the NME or ZTT. The Eighties simply stopped speaking with forked tongues – and got the knives out.

I was twenty-four in the summer of 1984, back in London after being married alive for five years in the home sweet home counties. And a far cry from the run-down, depressed, post-punk city I'd left, it was everything a great city should be: short-tempered, nasty and British, with careers starting to loom over the skyline like King Kong ravishing Manhattan. Medialand and West Wonderland were being written up in the glossies and the Sundays, and they both revolved around the Groucho, which had just opened. Every night, a man would walk through the bar and into the dining room, and the whole club would be hushed mid-hustle as a hundred eyes followed his progress. Then as he vanished, a rippling whisper would sashay through the spritzers: 'THAT'S THE MAN WHO FINISHED SOMETHING!'

In those years, projects, plans, CVs and calling cards

filled the Soho sky like tickertape greeting Charles Lindbergh. London had more egomaniacs, monomaniacs, nymphomaniacs, dipsomaniacs, dreamers and deranged than any city in the world, including New York. But what made it different, and special, and even lovable was that most of the people playing the game were only half serious. The whole hustle was played out with a theatrical and self-conscious obsessiveness that verged on parody; we were playing Manhattan in the Fifties, with much talk of *losers*, being *finished in this town*, being *wiped off the board*, the *A Party* and *Mr Nobody with a one-way ticket to Nowheresville*.

We had all read *What Makes Sammy Run?* (a friend of mine lent it to a boy who handed it back a week later and said with a straight face that it was the best Self-Help/Help-Yourself manual he'd ever read); we had all seen *The Sweet Smell Of Success* so many times we were muttering, 'Light me, Sidney!' in our sleep.

But more than anything, we were McLaren's Children. We had all been dreaming teens when Malcolm's finest moment was going through its paces and jumping through its hoops on prime-time slo mo. This, much more than being Thatcher's Children – though they turned out to be pretty much the same thing – would dog the rest of our working lives.

These days, desperate hippies with haircuts try to rewrite and reclaim punk as the last gasp of Right-On rebellion. But it wasn't. It *was* rebellious – but only in the way that Mrs Thatcher was. Punk was about a break with consensus. And we media brats, like our susser soulmates who would come up a few years later in the City – the Big Bang Boys, which in itself sounds like a McLaren concept group – were McLaren's *and* Thatcher's children. As the action moved from Roxyland to West Wonderland to EC Moneyland, we were still non-U upstarts with names like Steve and Paul and Julie and Debbie. What we all shared was Attitude; short-haired, impatient, get-filthy-rich-quick, liberal-baiting and hippie-hating.

This is what McLaren bequeathed to the world, and it was enough. Forgive him his projects, for he knows not what he does, and creativity has become a nervous tic with him – I mean, 'Vogueing'; what could be more appropriate for a man whose career has been standing still for the past ten years? But he was our wet nurse, and liquid gold ran from his breasts, and for this he deserves the respect that you would give a mother. For we are all of us McLaren's Children now.

Those years were important because they marked the last time that the Hip was really at home in the modern world. They rushed in where Trad Left and highbrow feared to tread – be bold, be bold, but not *too* bold! – celebrating the ephemeral, the possibilities and products of the new industries, the importance of style and taste and the new freedoms offered by cultural confusion.

We were in a *freefall* – a few truly modern souls, such as myself, revelled in the chance to live life at this most gorgeously chaotic of new frontiers, where nothing seems certain any more. But this attitude takes a strong stomach and a stiff upper lip, and for the most part hipsters – mostly white and male – couldn't take it, fake it or make it. There was a gradual realization that cultural freefall would have losers as well as winners; and for the first time, the losers looked highly likely to be white and male, for a change.

Well, we can't have that, can we, John? It was amusing to watch how, suddenly, hipsters and Right-Ons became such finicky eaters, socially speaking, leaving everything that came about after 1945 on the side of their plate for Mr Manners. Did we say we wanted freedom, social mobility and change? – sorry, could we have continuity, community and conservation instead, please?

Whether it was that arch-snob and phoney John Mortimer drivelling on about the glory days of the *noblesse oblige* Macmillan government, or Baroness Warnock being made 'physically sick' by a television report showing Mrs Thatcher buying off the peg at M&S or the *Arena* Jocko L'Homo boys whingeing on in perfect parodies of A. N. Wilson (who had just announced his intention to vote Labour for more social stability) Whyohwhynia about the 'orrendous break-up of community and all these Yuppies being *allowed* to buy *property* in *cities* (an *amazing* liberty, no? – especially when self-same hacks were sitting on nice little earners in Hampstead (Neil Spencer) and Highbury (Tony Parsons); what makes it sound for journalists from outside of London to come in and buy properties from indigenous Londoners, but not for bankers to? Answers on a pinhead, please), what it added up to was a bad case of the revisionisms, and a new world view which owed a lot more to Prince Charles (let's keep things as they are) than to Prince Nelson (let's tear the roof off the sucker and see what comes down).

'I'm so tired of fashion,' says McLaren now. 'Among the real hipsters in New York, London, Paris and Milan, it's hip to be unhip. It's *very* fashionable to be unfashionable.'

Next was the nemesis; the marginal world of Hip, which sought originally to sell on its own terms to the mainstream, has been conquered and consumed by it, seeing its finest moments regurgitated as fodder for advertising and the Sunday supps. Thus the hipsters are battening the hatches, shutting the shutters and staying at home with their Music For Pleasure LPs ('I hate pop') and their lawfully-wedded wives ('Shacking up is *so* tacky'). Couch cred ('I never go out any more') has replaced street cred as the mark of the true blue modern.

Which, as a leisure option, is fine; only a hyperactive eunuch would prefer to go out and dance than stay at home with something fuckable on the sofa and Dionne Warwick on the Dansette. But this is a choice based on pleasure, not principle; it is when we attempt to invest such choices with a moral dimension that we fall into the trap that plagues pundits and writers on the modern condition today. And that is that the modern – urban, changing – world is an evil place, and that fashion and *style* (there, said it) dot the i's and cross the t's of the case against compassion. 'You want style?' bellows Tony Parsons in *Arena* of all places. 'Thatcher is pure style.' Bollocks, Tone.

To claim that style has been corrupted by its Eighties association with status is to forget that style has *always* been about status, whether it was the dandy wishing to *épater le bourgeois* or the Mods dressing to create their own statusphere. It is pointless to rage against style because there *is no* golden pre-style age we can return to. Anti-style is just another stylistic option.

The sad fact is that the hip have turned on style not because it is a Thatcherite method of divisive elitism – but because it is now not elitist *enough*. There is no society less egalitarian than hip society, whose very basis lies in exclusivity. 'Neil's always buying designer clothes!'

burbles Chris Lowe of his fellow Pet Shop Boy. 'And then he never wears the stuff, because everyone else is!' Yes, *we* see; *I* express my personality through the clothes I choose, *you* shop, *they* consume.

Two maps of the modern world: for those at home in it, the map says YOU ARE HERE, and that's all we need; for the frightened, the map says, in the Medieval manner, HERE BE DRAGONNES. But how you gonna keep them down on the farm – sorry, 'rural community' – now that they've seen the Café de Paris?

From the great liners to the great bylines, the cry comes down this incredible, inedible century – ALL ABOARD THAT'S COMING ABOARD. Are *you* on for a one-way trip to the New World? No, things will never be certain again – no matter how many Richard Ford novels you read, or how many Scottish realist paintings of manual workers you look at, or how many boxing matches you attend. We are one nation in a freefall now – and about time too.

The escape from community and continuity and conservation, the whole Holy Grail that the zeitgeist of the twentieth-century express sought as it screamed like a bolshy banshee from station to station, is here at last. Which is not to say that things are perfect – but to recognize the value of social and cultural changes that will continue to open up, evolve and flourish whatever the complexion of government.

Don't try to fight it, because you'll be the loser. People have dreamed and died and worked their minds to distraction to make us this lonely, this free, and the least we owe them is enjoyment. To change the modern world, you must first learn to love it.

CHIC

. . . .

Chic – the very *word* begs a 'sic' these days – was invented in 1910 by the Tzarina Alix visiting the court of Kaiser Wilhelm, and smothered to death by the French, those notorious one-trick phoneys who possess the sad knack of mummifying anything they put their garlicky gloves on, in the Sixties. The corpse has been kicked about a bit since then, most notably by such high-yellow empresses as Bianca Jagger and Sade Adu – complex, completely contemporary women seeking to use classicism as decoy drag, just like Ferry at the mercy of his tuxedo's function – but everyone knows it's a dead word, like 'beverage'. It's only kept in usage for the benefit of the fashion editors, girls who just want to have puns – The Chic of Araby; The Chic Shall Inherit the Earth; Tongue in Chic – heh, heh. Yes, we see. (Nurse, the Letraset.)

But as a living alternative, chic really is dead, consigned to the dirty old dressing-up box of history – until Vivienne Westwood revives it, like the bustle, for two weeks in twenty years' time. At its best and stripped to its barest bones, chic was about black, boyishness and breeding; the Tzarina Alix got it in one when, at a time when fashionable women wore lilac, sea-green and hats featuring whole egrets frozen in death with outstretched wings, she turned up at Kaiser Bill's wearing a man's black suit with a collar and black tie. That evening she wore the original little black dress, when black was a colour only for mourning, high at the neck, when the fashion favoured acres of décolletage, with one Russian Order of Merit on the chest. The black and the red; she could have stepped out of the Moscow Club.

Tzarina Alix obviously knew that chic is never about sex. On the contrary, chic is beauty with all the sex, sweat and seed sucked out, the dry husk of lust. Women dress with chic for other women because men, give or take a few brownie hounds and gridniks, don't go for that at all. The chicest women are often the ugliest: think of Wallis Simpson, Diana Vreeland.

Sex symbols are never chic; it was a favourite device of Hollywood, back in the days when they still used women, to set a sexy girl against a chic one and let them battle over some hunk – Gardner vs Kelly in *Mogambo*, Harlow vs Astor in *Red Dust*, Crawford vs Shearer in *The Women*, Elizabeth Taylor vs Dina Merrill in *Butterfield 8*. The least chic female celebrity these days is probably the unimpeachably sexy Madonna, who took up the gold lamé flag from Elizabeth Taylor, who herself bore the greatest beauty man ever set eye on like an open wound and never ever learned to put one sartorial foot in front of the platform-soled other. Money can't buy you chic; in her great book *Who's Afraid Of Elizabeth Taylor?*, Brenda Maddox describes the gory scene when Miss Taylor's million-dollar mistakes arrived at the home of Richard Burton's God-fearing middle-aged sisters in the small Welsh town of Pontrhydyfen:

'Elizabeth sends trunks full of clothes,' says Mrs Owen. She runs upstairs to fetch an armful. The sight is incredible; those hideous movie queen gowns from the news photos spread out over the Welsh cretonne sofa. They are short and wide, almost square. There was a black and white silk from the days of the mini skirt, its brief length made even shorter by the low square neck and the thick velvet belt and the large print on the fabric. There were silver sequins on blue silk, and fuchsia and yellow kaftans from Robinson's of Beverly Hills. 'She loves kaftans,' said Mrs Owen.

Elsewhere her friend Elliott Kastner groaned, 'Simpli-city, Elizabeth! . . . Elizabeth's taste is all in her mouth. If she were low key, she'd leave Kelly in the dust.'

Elizabeth Taylor didn't need chic: she had her diamonds, her spades, her clubs and her hearts – she was, as one of her earlier films pointed out, *The Girl Who Had Everything*. A girl with no chic and no nothing was Marilyn Monroe, teen angel cheerleader of the walking wounded, who in the dog-end days of her life found herself pitted against the First Lady of chic and America, Jacqueline Bouvier Kennedy, more poignantly and hurtfully than any doxie vs deb scenario. It was MM who called JBK 'the Statue – I bet he doesn't put his hand up *her* dress', and JBK who confirmed this by telling a friend that sex was a bad thing – 'it wrinkles the clothes'.

Jackie Kennedy was a snob; an Un-American and proud of it, her indictable activities included calling the tenants from whom she expropriated the White House 'Colonel Cornpone and his little pork chop' (Colonel and Mamie Eisenhower to *vous*) and leaning as surely as the Tower of Pisa towards the couturiers of France, buying from

Molyneux, Balenciaga, Givenchy and Cardin, causing a patriotic furore over the *wagons-lits* of francs frittered away on French frocks: 'I couldn't spend *that* much unless I wore sable underwear!'

Later, like a parable by Oscar Wilde, the statue broke down and screamed, 'My God, what are they doing? My God, they've killed Jack, they've killed my husband, Jack, Jack,' when fairytale met reality – Paris vs Texas – chic by jowl and blood the colour of her Revlon Tender Red lipstick covered her Chanel suit.

But that was in the scarlet-drenched Sixties; in the sugar-pink Fifties, when JFK married his French-speaking debutante and Grace Kelly married her Frog prince and Gene Kelly and Audrey Hepburn used the Champs-Elysées as a back-lit back lot, chic became a Franco-American affair. Jacqueline Kennedy was a Bouvier, and her rangy body spoke an international language which whispered to a wide-eyed world that the French and chic were now as inextricably linked as the French and cowardice, croissants and collaboration.

The English flirted with it briefly in the pages of *Queen About Town* – think of Barbara Goalen, Fiona Campbell Walter, Kay Kendall – but they always had too much of a sense of humour: think of Kendall in *Genevieve*, the picture of *sang froid* jumping up and playing the trumpet in a dive, her designer TB cheeks blowing out like those of a poison puffer fish. Chic thrives on poker-faced nostalgia, which the French and Americans have in common, always looking over the cold shoulder to a time when they ruled the world and *what's more* no one cracked jokes about them.

Thus, taking its cue from a time when the chicest woman of the Twenties had been the French-born star of American films, Claudette Colbert, chic mutated for the final time – not the Trans-Europe transvestite ruling-class games of Tzarina Alix or the stern, thrilling *arriviste* King-making eccentricity of Simpson and Vreeland. Givenchy created L'Interdit for Hepburn, Molyneux created Vivre for Kelly, and chic was now a strictly bourgeois mixture of American arrogance and French frigidity. Some of the chicest women of the Fifties were the Hitchcock girls, Hedren, Kelly and Sainte, sinners by omission tortured time and time again for their coldness, their cunning and their *chic*.

Babbitt on the boulevard; hence in the Fifties, 'Paris *is* the American Dream', said (arrogant, frigid) Gertrude Stein. By 1986, Robert Elms had a better way of saying it: 'Paris is the paradise of the easily-impressed – the universal provincial mind.' Americans were rarely described better. This being so it is hardly surprising that the French vanguard, a po-faced lot at the best of times, did not take kindly to clean-cut and cute Audrey Hepburn prancing around their precious (in both senses of the word) *boîtes* and basements in her cheapo Edith Head copy of Juliette Greco's Balmain ('a blackboard which gave full rein to the imagination') for the blind glass eye of Avedon-Astaire in *Funny Face*. These Americans – they thought existentialism meant adding rooms on to your house!

Sulking, the self-elected reps of French beatnik chic went to earth on the Left Bank, finding a des res on Saint Germain des Prés, producing their own monochrome icons to combat Hollywood's Technicolor cluelessness – Greco, of the much-publicized just-good-friendship with Brando, Françoise Sagan of the purple prose, Anouk Aimée of the black dress and black eye. Chic went through the Left Bank like a bromide and came out Breathless with post-coital Tristesse.

When it comes to popular culture, the French are as incapable of progressing as they are of calling *la Manche* the English Channel. Couture houses founded in the Twenties still rule the paltry roost in a business founded on fickleness. They are still making *nouvelle vague* films, all meaningful glances, mirthless laughter, *amour fou* and police in leather jackets chasing people in the Metro – all filmed with the camera held between the cameraman's legs, *naturellement*. They are still jazzzzz bores *par excellence*, bar none. Johnny Halliday still gets to number one on the singles chart, despite being over fifty. How can you even try to drag a country into the twentieth century when only this year their Minister of Culture went on the radio to call Mick Jagger 'a threat to the family'? As any English first-former could tell you, Mick Jagger *is* the family.

Like all causes the French take up, chic died in their arms as surely as Mimi died in Rudolfo's. Greco, for all her rarefied air, let a senile Darryl Zanuck take her off to Hollywood, where she quickly proved to be box office poison. Swinging Londres was just around the corner, and its blatancy made French suggestiveness look archaic; faced with Julie Christie's blank, frank, unbearably sexy stare, Leslie Caron's coquettishness looked like something straight out of *la belle époque*.

'Paris is like a fifty-year-old virgin chattering on about the joys of sexual intercourse,' sneered Joe Orton in the Sixties. It was with the knock-kneed schoolgirl gawk of the mini that chic as a design for dressing finally became an essentially *matronly* affair. Joseph, unimpeachably French, said it well: 'Paris is not *dull*, exactly . . . but it is *classic*, which makes it less alive. London isn't yet a museum, things happen.' Jasper Conran provided a blunter interpretation: 'Chic . . . that's a vile, horrible, silly word. Well, it's French, isn't it? They're *full* of shit.'

Full of *chic*, did he say? No, all that's left of that are the names of the saints – Saint Laurent, Saint Chanel, Saint Dior. These names mean little to the girl on the sidewalk and even less to the girls on the catwalk who moan to a man about the bad pay and predictability of Paris fashion. The phantoms of the French soap opera float on, but everyone knows they died with chic, somewhere in the Sixties. Till Sade's next sleeve kicks the corpse around once more; chic, rest in pieces.

GOODBYE CRUEL WORLD:
Y.O.U., M.E. AND THE DISCREET CHARM
OF COCOONING

. . . .

Tired? Lethargic? Can't get out of bed and don't *want* to go outside the door? Cheer up. You probably think you've got M.E. – the AIDS of the chattering classes. But what you've *probably* got is Y.O.U.

Consider: last year the restaurant business proper grew by half a per cent. Restaurant food *to go*, on the other hand, grew by *nine* per cent. And we're not talking fast fodder for the masses here; we're talking burghers with an H. We're talking about the Dining Car, which will bring you dinner from Mijanou, La Bastide and a handful of other West Wonderland gaffs specializing in creative ways to serve up an arm and a leg.

Of course, food to go has always had a caste system: champagne breakfasts in bed and sushi boxes at the office have been around for years. But the first is about luxury, and the second about practicality; their point is to save a marriage, or save time. The delivery of gourmet dinners for one from restaurants whose very ambience and high publicity profile was supposed to be a good part of the pleasure of eating there; this is a new thing. 'Anditsalittlebitscary!' as Peter York used to say.

So what does it mean, that a thousand dispatch riders

are at this moment thundering across London with terrine of aubergine, *fritto misto* and pork with prunes and Armagnac bouncing biliously in their boxes, heading for stomachs who can stomach anything but the thought of eating with Other People?

Does it indicate the same malaise which has opened its wings over the nation's starlets, who now share something more than a liking for the frocks of Miss Lolita Lempicka? 'Dan and I are very domestic; we never go out' (Patsy Kensit); 'I hate going out. My idea of heaven is a bare room with two huge speakers' (Gina Bellman); 'I don't go clubbing; I like to read a lot, mainly classics. My favourite is Balzac; *Père Goriot* gets me going far more than any club I've ever been to' (Felly of Techtronic). Does it mean that for the first time in their recorded history – in the gossip columns – the Going Out classes (young, affluent, hedonistic) are Staying In? Yes.

Staying in has become the measure of the modern. How many nights a week you can manage it has replaced hard clubbing as your proof of bonding with the *zeitgeist*. Even those who find it hard to give up going out still *claim* that they never do it any more, and will come up with a brace of brazen alibis should you tell them that the cube friend of a friend saw them at the Lizard Lounge last week. 'Oh, my cousin was over from Holland – I promised to show her a good time. Well, (snigger) what the *Euros* think of as a good time. You know me – I never go out these days.' Lying bitch.

In the past, especially in America, otherwise sane people in cities and suburbs, in bachelor flats and bunk bedrooms, would turn off the light on a Saturday night and sit immobile in the dark rather than let anyone know they were in. Now, being found in a nightclub on a

Saturday night is more than your media job's worth; it gives the phrase *getting caught out* a whole new meaning.

Curiously, the phenomenon was first sighted in America, the country where unpopularity is feared as much as Communism, and where an all-purpose beano for businessmen is quite appropriately called a 'convention'; wanting to be alone is supremely Un-American, and may explain why Garbo was always much bigger in Europe. In the late Eighties, young hedonists started to take root – an occurrence which was christened, with typical inelegance, couch-potatoing, and involved a lot of beer, a stack of dirty videos and a gaggle of young men whose table manners would make the late John Belushi look like Joanna Lumley. Few things are as squalid as the sight of surplus men at ease.

But couch-potatoing was followed quickly by a more salubrious twist on staying put: cocooning. And cocooning had status; it was less cathode-orientated and more Eurosmoochy, involving at least two people of at least two sexes. Cocooning is the cocaine of cohabitation, inducing an unimpeachable sense of superiority and well-being. It is also addictive, and in 1989 Nancy Popcorn – the American one-woman Henley Centre – predicted that cocooning would be *the* great social wave of the Nineties, completely deconstructing and redefining the whole industries of catering, entertainment and leisure. The ugly duckling of unpopularity had become the swan of exclusivity – excluding everything outside your own front door.

So far, so soft focus; cocooning as a sensible and self-protective response to the harshness and stress of the rat race. This sounds nicely vague and blame-free: *society did it, your Honour – made me stay in with my main squeeze and get insensible on Krug and pizza!* But the sticky sticking point remains that life was actually much harsher and more stressful in the past, during the Depression and the Recession, and in other countries. It is a monumentally racist and élitist white lie that only Western late twentieth-century city-dwelling professionals suffer from stress. But, in the past, the harder life got the more people felt the need for the company and solace of strangers.

So is there another explanation for this sudden outbreak of cocooning? A reason, perhaps, that dare not whisper its name for fear of treading on toes? I believe so. It is a strange coincidence that cocooning was spotted around the time that M.E. – the Undisease that leaves you down, out and wondering what it's all about, Alfredo – hit home, leaving hordes of Undead hotshots in its wake; Hurricane Me! I believe that M.E. and cocooning are expressions of the same malaise – a deep and profound boredom verging on the clinical and encompassing the physical. And here's the rub: people are not bored with themselves (that's old-fashioned depression, and that old tart's not the belle of *anyone's* 'Come As The Sick Soul Of Europe' fin-de-siècle ball) but with other people. To put it plainly – what's wrong with me isn't M.E.: it's Y.O.U.

The average moderately social being, as the Nineties go into the opening moves of the modern manners minuet, feels like a girl who in a fit of high spirits has volunteered to be on the receiving end of a sex train (gang bang to you oiks) and two hours later is regretting it. NOT YOU AGAIN! – DIDN'T I JUST SEE *YOU*? NOT YOU, TOO! I THOUGHT I'D SEEN THE LAST OF *YOU*. That's Y.O.U. for you.

We are socially fatigued – fucked out. Our *bons mots* drop like lead balloons, and we clutch our martinis like Mae West life-jackets. Our dreams of the wit and wonder of the Algonquin were meant to come true here at the Groucho, but we've started to realize we had more fun fifteen years ago getting legless on Pernod and black at Shitshire's hottest nite-spot. Beam me up, Dottie.

We are sick and tired of laboured dinner party conversations – a dinner party is a party with everything that made parties great taken out – and exhausted with modelling our wit, charm and personality as though they were designer garments we were trying to flog to rich widows: life as a catwalk. 'Everybody is somebody's bore,' said Edith Sitwell. But, please God, why did you in your wisdom decide to let me have the pleasure of meeting all of them before my young life was through?

'Boredom is, after all, a form of criticism,' said William Phillips in *Sense Of The Present*. This is why no one has dared – up till *now*, heh heh – connect cocooning and boredom. To be bored is to commit a value judgement, which is considered marginally worse than cage-fighting these days. A person who is openly bored and not ashamed of showing it has a bloodcurdling advantage over his peers; he is armed, to draw both blood and crowds. When we are bored by someone, we become whether we mean to or not their very own Butcher of Broadway; we have reviewed their unique personhood, this big thing in their lives – their self – and found it sadly wanting. We don't demand an encore, we just turn mystified to our mutual friend – *is that all there is?* And like Frank Rich himself, if we can put together a critique that cuts like a chiv and sparkles like champagne – for nothing wounds like wit – and get it to the ears of the right people, we can get their show off the road once and forever and kill them dead as vaudeville. We probably wouldn't even *mean* to; but, friends, it can be done.

We live in a world where being called a bore is worse than being called an adulterer, a dipsomaniac, a nymphomaniac or lower middle class. We are as superstitious as actors just out of RADA in *Macbeth*, feeling that if it is so much as mentioned by name, it will spread like bushfire. (As teenagers, contrarily, when boredom is as remote as death itself, we *pretend* to be bored incessantly; I used to wear a badge pronouncing BORED TEENAGER to a yawning world.) See no boredom, hear no boredom, speak no boredom; running scared and playing dirty, we stoop so low as to insinuate that if someone is bored, they are *themselves* boring. He who smelt it dealt it, as the Lads used to say.

We bottle it up and throw it out to sea with a note in it saying 'HELP! – HELD PRISONER BY BORES!' We put it under our pillow and hope that the Bored-To-The-Back-Tooth Fairy will take it away and leave a pretty credit card in its place. But oh, how it takes its toll. And the price at that phantom tollbooth is what we're paying now, in fatigue and exhaustion, in couching and cocooning, in M.E. and Y.O.U., in the sour taste that hip hosannas leave in our mouths. BEEN THERE DONE THAT. SEE YOU ANON. LET'S HAVE LUNCH. How sadly, like flat champagne on a monumental Morning After, they contrast with the hellzapopping greetings of the past: WHAT'S HAPPENING? WHAT'S THE STORY? WHERE'S THE ACTION? Modern salutations never end in question marks: we already know the answers.

Well, *are* people more boring than they used to be? It

could be so, but I find it more likely that the mode of friendship, rather than of friends themselves, has degenerated. The Sixties ruined a lot of things – sex, drugs, trousers and the work of Jim Webb – and they also might have ruined friendship by bringing instant intimacy and psychobabble frankness on to the scene. These things have taken the spice and the simmering out of soul-baring: those Victorian friendships where people addressed each other formally for the first twenty years, and a person was a Pass The Parcel with numerous tantalizing layers to be peeled away before the raw, squirming thing at the centre was revealed. Just think, you could have twenty years of foreplay! (Nice work if you can get it!) But lack of formality and reserve means that friends inevitably get used up a lot quicker than they used to. Though when we have sucked them dry, we're not allowed to throw the skin away; friendship is the new sacred cow, and you take a raincheck on her milk of human kindness at your peril.

'Here they come at midnight,' wrote clever Mr Nietzsche, 'Tapping on my windows, crying "Let me in!" – the ghosts of my abandoned friends.' As we break free from the bonds of the family, we wrap around ourselves the octopus of friendship instead; shedding a friend is now more shameful than shedding a spouse or a widowed, white-haired old mother in many circles. But if we are alive, we are changing, and no friend can hold us without holding us down.

A mystique, a new religion almost, has grown up around friendship. It has been given a dignity and a classicism that other relationships – marriage, family – have had mercilessly stripped from them over the past century. But friendship is as random and illogical as everything else; as Peter Ustinov said, 'Friends are not necessarily the people you like best; they are merely the people who got there first.' The fear lurks in all our minds: dear God, what if there was queue-jumping? WE MIGHT HAVE BEEN DONE OUT OF KEANU REEVES AND KIM BASINGER!

So, in the end, we get not the friends that we deserve but the ones who get there on time. And do we really like them as much as we say? Are they really such a big noise? Personality has been democratized under the American influence of the last fifty years, and we now believe rather stupidly and sentimentally that everyone is a valuable and unique human being. Not so: we meet two dozen wonderful people in a lifetime, and the rest are spiritual birdseed.

We pretend that everyone we know is brilliant, beautiful and fascinating, because if they're not, what does that say about *us*? That we hang out with *nerds*? Takes one to know one. Whereas we with Y.O.U. have turned our backs on such panics. 'I always thought, all my life, that somewhere there was this most wonderful party in the world which I wasn't being asked to,' said a young Cambridge friend of mine. 'And when I started moving up the ladder, and I started going to parties that got featured in the *Tatler*, I *still* had that feeling. One New Year's Night, I was in the Café de Paris and I was next to Sade in the "Auld Lang Syne" circle. As she kissed me, again I had this flash – there's a better party somewhere. I know it sounds dumb. But then, when I moved into this houseful of old Etonians in Cambridge, I understood why I never found the party. The golden group, the real movers, just don't go out. Every day the invitations come up from London and they just snigger and throw them in the bin. Then they sit on the sofa all night watching tapes of *Neighbours*. It's a very rarefied world.'

From the sublime to the Slimline Tonic set, it is interesting that beautiful young women – the Mandies and Patsies who would have been the definitive dollies in the Sixties – marry so young these days. Back then, your Judies and Julies stayed single forever, wringing out every last drop that life, love and Swinging London had to offer. But now it's a quick once round the block and they're married before they can vote: been there, done that. Work it out, use it up – then time to go home. Not to Mother, but to Daddy.

Once, only the rich had social lives as such; now everyone does, and there are too many bozos in the Sun-supp photos, too many B&T types going AWOL. The crowning of Wednesday night as *the* night at the Café de Paris in 1986 was an early warning of Y.O.U. – the Cubes had to be at work next day, and thus wouldn't show up to show out in your floorspace. You start off avoiding the hoi polloi – you end up avoiding your best friend. But such is Y.O.U.

So what are we going to do about Y.O.U? Coast. Cruise. Enjoy, enjoy. Centuries of indoctrination have convinced us that one is a lonely number, but it just isn't so. There is a pure sensual appeal to being alone that cannot be translated into a social setting without a terrible breach of decent manners. For instance, in the brilliant *Sammy And Rosie Get Laid*, there is a scene wherein Sammy snorts cocaine, drinks a milkshake, wolfs a cheeseburger, watches television and listens to Mozart on his Walkman ALL AT ONCE. Can you imagine being allowed to commit such sensory overload in society, where pleasures are rationed and rational, where there is no place for the self-indulgent satyr, where you have to PASS THE PORT? But who in hell wants to pass the port WHEN YOU CAN DRINK IT ALL YOURSELF?

Maybe we cats who walk alone are selfish, smug and verging on the psychopathic. But I think it more likely that we are simply returning to our roots. Most sensitive people were born again in their thirteenth year in the sweltering solitude of their bedroom during the long hot summer holiday; while making friends was a deviation, going it alone feels like going home. Be my witness, Garbo, Monroe, Bardot – and Morrissey, Frown Prince of Y.O.U. Pop.

Although in a way I admire those who still See People – there is something touchingly hopeful and hearty about them, forever hacking it on an after-dark Duke of Edinburgh Outward Bound Scheme – I can't help wondering what they're looking for. Some sort of new life form? And I can't help despising their naivety, their programmed adherence to a social life that no longer satisfies or stimulates them.

And I can't help thinking that we who want to be alone are more complete. 'Misery loves company', but happiness doesn't feel on the shelf by itself. I believe that those people who crave society can't stand being alone with themselves for fear of what they'll find. Be bold, be bold, but not *too* bold – there is no Bluebeard's locked room so fearful as the face in the mirror.

CAUSE FOR CONCERN

. . . .

Remember Ronald Reagan? The brain that launched a thousand quips? One of the lighter features of his presidency, I always thought, was the marked difference in attitude towards him from the LSE – Liberal Showbiz Establishment – on either side of the Atlantic.

In this corner, led by honorary Euro Gore Vidal, the most important thing about Reagan, it seemed, was that *he had once been an actor!* Yes – a lowly hawker of his wares in the bazaars of Thespis Street! 'The Acting President', Vidal liked to call him – over and over again, as it turned out. And the inference was that anybody who had been an actor, for any period of time – despite the fact that Reagan had rallied the hordes for at least twice as long as he'd trodden the boards – was unfit to hold political office. The Scarlet Letter revisited; 'A' not for 'Adulterer', but for 'Actor'!

This cry was taken up by the alt coms – Benny and Jenny and Lenny and Dawn – who would bang on about Reagan being an actor – nudge nudge, wink wink – and then turn around and harangue the audience for three hours solid about the situation in Nicaragua/Namibia/Northern Ireland, and how the politicians were too stupid to sort it out! Not like Benny and Jenny, who'd have the whole kit and caboodle sorted out toot sweet if only the bloody politicians would move over and give them a go. Remember the stories about Stephen Fry coaching Neil Kinnock?

The Petitioners, I called them; they were so addicted to signing things that they'd have signed their own death warrant if it had been pushed under their nose by someone wearing the right badge. For some reason I never worked out, it was okay for a *comic* to be a political animal – but an *actor*?

But from the LSE of America came silence. Because even though all those limousine liberals and Malibu Marxists didn't *like* Reagan, they didn't mind the fact that he'd been an actor. Truth to tell, they were well chuffed; all the easier for Warren, Robert or Michael Douglas when their turn came.

British entertainers – until the Kinnock-Spawn – have never been political; whoever knew what Olivier thought about Suez? Even the Rolling Stones' much-touted rebellion came down to Jagger having the hots for Angela Davis, and Tom Driberg having the hots for Jagger. As old Lilo Lips summed it up himself: 'My heart is Labour, my brain is Liberal – but my money is Tory.' Dressing to the left was only ever a dance craze on this side of the pond.

British actors, especially, approached their politics as they approached their divorces – with discretion. But in America the political affiliations of the celebrity have been in the window for a long time, along with the state of their marriages and their mental health. Why the difference?

Most likely, I believe, is the desire of the American actor

to feel like a *whole* person – or *poisson*, as they say. Politics, like his shrink and his divorces, make him feel well-rounded, real. All the terrible problems of Americans are magnified in their biggest stars, unlike Europe. The biggest American is the *saddest* American: Marilyn, Elvis, James Dean. There is no such thing as a happy American. No people who feel okay would bang on about being a 'person' as much as Americans do (what else can one be, the European wonders?) or spend so much time and money trying to 'find' oneself. If one has to find oneself, then oneself must be – or at least feel – *lost*.

Zelda Fitzgerald perfectly described the American phenomenon of Person-Panic in her short story 'The Original Follies Girl', as an ageing actress takes stock of her life:

> At this time she was making an awful struggle to hang on to something that had never crystallised for her – it was the past. She wanted to get her hands on something tangible, to be able to say 'That is real, that is part of my experience, that goes into this or that category, this that happened to me is part of my memories.' She could not correlate the events that made up her life, so now she was beginning to feel time passing she felt as though she had just been born. The isolation of each day made her incapable of feeling surprise and caused her to be wonderfully tolerant – which is another way of saying she was sick with spiritual boredom.

Some eight years ago, I asked Peter York why the Americans made films like *Texas Chainsaw Massacre*, and he said, quick as a flash: 'It's because the houses went up too fast!' I pretended I understood, even though I didn't. Now I think I do: it's all to do with this lost sense of self, and this endless toleration which leads to self-sickness.

So the American actor – being the most visible American, with the greatest fear of being found invisible – clothes the disappearing self in causes. In the Sixties, ethnic dressing was in – the Viet Cong and the Black Panthers. But by the Seventies, with psychoanalysis in full swing, such stands became a little too outward-looking to feel real. Reality was, after all, just a diversion from the real; looking for Mr Self. 'The tolerant Pacific air,' wrote Auden of Hollywood, 'makes logic seem so silly, pain/Subjective'. Liberal isolationism followed, and the concerns were for the American Indian and nuclear reactors. And then the plight of the small farmer.

It was here that the naivety and insensitivity of the LSE reached a point of no return. In an interesting twist on the thespian habit of falling in love with the leading man for the duration of the shoot, Sissy Spacek, Sally Field and Jessica Lange made films about the plight of the small farmer and promptly began to speak at *real* rallies. But, of course, it ended in tears; many of the farmers turned out to be rabid rednecks who blamed not Reagan but the Jews for their plight, and the films died a death. It would be charitable to believe it was the first surprise, rather than the second, which led to the farmers being cast aside like so many human hula-hoops; redundant once more.

This episode seemed all the more amazing because these actresses had actually grown up in such communities, and always made a point of speaking of their abject misery there – and got out to New York or

Europe as soon as humanly possible. If a way of life is so loathsome, why fight to preserve it? I'll tell you why: because the noble savages they had found in their scripts had *obscured* the reality of their early experiences; the fiction had won out over the facts of life. Few things demonstrate the entertainer's tenuous grasp on reality more starkly than this rude awakening; an inability to differentiate between fact and fiction being, ironically, a charge which actors habitually level at their audiences.

Bob Geldof writes brilliantly of the monumental selfishness and America Firstness of this supposedly 'liberal' cause when he describes Bob Dylan – a Jewish boy who grew up in Minnesota and experienced chilling anti-Semitism, running away to New York eight times before the age of sixteen – finishing up the American end of the Live Aid show:

The biggest disappointment of the evening was Dylan; the performance was catastrophic. He was out of time, couldn't stay in tune and seemed to treat the songs with disdain. Then he displayed a complete lack of understanding of the issues raised by saying, unforgivably, 'It would be nice if some of the money went to American farmers.' Something so simplistic and crowd-pleasing was beyond belief; crass, stupid and nationalistic. Dylan left the stage, and as he looked up at his manager he just said 'Sorry'.

Indeed, the growth of narcissism and the lack of perspective of the supposedly liberal people involved could be seen during the recording of the American Band Aid record. While *Do They Know It's Christmas?* was in no doubt about who was in trouble and who was in clover, with its ceaseless pleas for 'them', the American response *We Are The World* (really? The world as America's back yard?) seemed only to feel concern for a cause that was 'us': 'We are the world, we are the children, we are the ones who make a brighter day . . . we're saving our own lives.'

You could hear more altruism in a Coca-Cola jingle.

It is almost too perfect that Greenery has become the final resting place of the LSE. Green politics, while masquerading as a desire to save the human race, is a scream of hate against a humanity who dared mess up this 'perfect' (hollow laugh) planet.

You are not a Vietnamese baby, or a Black Panther, or a small farmer, goes the new thinking: you are what you eat. It was somehow inevitable that the American liberal conscience would end up in its own bowels; in the belly of the beast itself. And so, while AIDS and crack consume the inner cities, Meryl Streep leads Mothers Against Pesticides and the LSE prepares for *The Earth Day Special* in which such towering intellects as Jack Nicholson, Bette Midler, Jane Fonda, Michael Douglas, Barbra Streisand, Bruce Willis, Chevy Chase, Dan Ackroyd, Streep and Sting (but of course) will tell us what's wrong with the world.

You do not have to be a modernist monster to feel that this smorgasbord of self-adoration not only has more to do with showing off than saving the world (though of course if *we are the world* then we're saving ourselves, which must make it pretty irresistible to these fucking boneheads), but that it's also proof that Gore Vidal was right: in fact, not only should actors be barred from office, but they should be stripped of their voting rights too.

But *why* do these people seem so morally repellent? In the past, actors who involved themselves with issues – Ava and Frankie stumping for Stevenson; Bogart and Bacall flying to the HUAC hearings on a plane called Red Star; Marilyn on the arm of Miller, smiling radiantly at the reporter who asked her what she thought about communists before replying, 'They're for the people, aren't they?' – seemed both glamorous and righteous. Why do political actors now come across as such self-serving hippies?

Try this. Somewhere in the Sixties, actors lost their self-loathing. The germs first introduced by Method went mainstream, and manured by pop psychology and free expression, actors began to perceive their game-playing as more real than real life. Traditionally, actors had little but contempt for themselves – the best ones, that is. 'This is no job for a man . . . we all despise ourselves, and that's why we drink': Richard Burton. 'I haven't done a damn thing that's worthwhile; I brought nothing to this business and I have no respect for it': Ava Gardner. 'There is no such thing as a great actor': Marlon Brando. 'My war work is the only worthwhile thing I've done in my life': Marlene Dietrich. 'Acting is not important – plumbing is': Spencer Tracy.

But far from destroying them, this clear-eyed evaluation of their talents seems to have made them what they were; greatness seems *only* to emerge from a cocoon of conflict and confusion. The creatures of the studio system were bullied and belittled ceaselessly by the bosses and directors but they emerged immortal. And immortality, *not* living well, is the best revenge.

These days, actors agonize over their piddling profession as though it was a cross between winning the

Second World War and working with lepers; acting is 'hell', 'a constant struggle', 'harder than a prizefight'. Yet paradoxically, they seem to find it singularly easy to master. One thinks of Monroe, merciless with herself until the end in her desire to be a good actress – 'What have I got? Big tits, big ass – big deal!' Then one thinks of Keaton, Lange, Turner and all, forever banging on about their plans to write, produce, direct. That *that* woman above all could think so little of herself, and these nobodies think so much; truly, there's no justice on this earth, and that's much sadder than dying forests.

The tormented, colossal stars are gone, replaced with a new race secure in the smug beliefs that acting is the hardest job on God's earth *and* that they're okay guys. They all have projects, land, children, causes; they are the Stepford Stars, the living equivalent of *thirtysomething* – caring, sharing, soul-baring and boring as all-get-out.

And it is because of their smugness that the politics of celebrity now stick in the craw; their self-satisfaction is such that their 'activism' seems like inactivism – like good cocaine, just another way of feeling good about yourself. Green politics, in the final analysis, is so popular with the rich because it contains no race or class analysis at all; politics with everything but the glow of involvement taken out. If anything, poor people can be charged with more pollution than the rich (convenience foods) and Third Worlders with more destruction than whites (the rainforests). It is the only analysis of the world's evils which leaves the rich untouched by guilt; and if *we* are the world, then Green is the logical outcome of narcissism and withdrawal – the ultimate *ME* movement.

William Hurt is sued for maintenance on TV; Robin Williams does a three-hour comic routine about his drug problem. But without secrecy, there can be no surprise; without surprise, no honesty. The final irony is that the Stepford Stars – forever pursuing their shadowy 'realness', forever in search of their lost selves – seem far *less* real than the creatures of the studio machine. The radiant reality and humanity of Marilyn Monroe will shine on this imperfect and beautiful planet long after the clowns who plan to bring us *The Earth Day Special* have gone the way of all flesh – and all forests.

LAD OVERBOARD

. . . .

With the sad death of Mr Gary Holton in 1985, an era came to an end. Not so much an era, actually, as a prolonged pub crawl, but there you go. The world didn't just lose an actor – it lost a Lad.

Holton was terminal Lad, Lad on the Rocks. Towards the end of his life he was such a royal pain, taking the Lad characteristics of drinking, arrogance and misbehaviour to their logical conclusion – complete and utter Prannethood – that even his fellow showbiz Lads, a tolerant lot, had begun to despise him.

His lack of professionalism, paedophile tendencies and treatment of his long-suffering girlfriend Sue (Lads always have long-suffering girlfriend Sues) had made him a Lad liability and he was on the point of being written out of the TV series *Auf Wiedersehen, Pet* – his first big break in more than fifteen years in showbusiness; each Lad kills the thing he loves, usually himself – when he sank his last bevvy. He was a Lad insane.

It was interesting to note that the parts which had gone previously to Mr Holton would now go by default to the young actor Phillip Daniels, the one forever urging you to make your hair colour a shade more daring. At last

126

Mr Daniels' refusal to risk making his career a shade more daring would pay off. You see, in recent years LadLand has been such a no-go zone that very few young actors have found it a profitable seam to mine.

The early Seventies, when Holton and Daniels were formed, were very Lad Heaven; Marji Wallace on the loose, La Valbonne not yet a byword of mirth, the *Confessions* films, Paul Raymond finding his feet, Fiona Richmond screwing her way around the world and writing up the results in *Men Only* (Richmond was an X-rated Monkees; if you're a Lad you'd better get ready, she might be coming to your town), Penthouse Pets and Playboy Clubs not yet despised warrens of C2s and campiness but something to aspire to.

In those days, you could be glad to be Lad.

The Lad was a true product of inflated leisure and affluence if ever there was one – it cost time and money being a Lad, what with all the booze that you ran on like petrol, and all the mornings-after off work with the collywobbles; try pulling *that* in a buyers' market. He came to frisky fruition throughout the Sixties, starting in a desperate, Northern, fatalistic sort of way – Albert Seaton in *Saturday Night And Sunday Morning* – and mutating into a strictly Southern phenomenon.

The South is the seat of showbiz, which is the Lad Olympus, after all, and the Southern working-class have a long and dishonourable tradition of making themselves over into cheeky monkeys to escape drudgery through entertainment (Max Miller, Tommy Trinder, music hall). Lad fitted in nicely with the idea of Swinging London, being saucy, sexy and tame, and was seen in action in films like *The Knack* and *Alfie*: but being very parochial, Lad only ever produced one specimen who translated into

127

TransAtlantic – Michael Caine, International Lad. (When Caine kissed Christopher Reeve full on the lips in *Deathtrap*, a product of the Emasculating Eighties, it was the Lad Altamont.)

But the Seventies were when every Lad had his leg over. Turn on the TV and they were there, in all their feather-cut glory: Richard O'Sullivan in *Man About The House*, Craven of *Please Sir!*, Adam Faith's *Budgie*. There were Lad pop stars: Rod Stewart, Ian Hunter, Phil Lynott, David Essex. Lads Own sporting heroes: Barry Sheene, James Hunt. Elder statesmen of Lad: Malcolm Allison (left his wife for Bunny Serena). Laugh-a-Minute Lads: Jim Davidson. And Lad lags: John Bindon, Ronald Biggs. These you have loved, if you're a Lad.

The Seventies also produced the only two geniuses ever to verge on Lad-dom: Tom Jones and George Best, though discovered in the Sixties, only came into their own – and everybody elses – in the Seventies. They did all a Junior League Lad dreams of in his wildest, wettest dreams – dated beauty queens, fathered boy children, knew that they could lick any girl in the room when they walked into Tramp – but somehow they were just too talented to be Lads Proper. You have to have a large element of mediocrity in your make-up to be a Lad, and Best and Jones were just too good at what they did. A genius cannot be a Lad, and vice versa.

The Seventies, golden age of Lad. Note: a Lad is not a Playboy – Victor A. Lownes III and Porfirio Rubirosa were not Lads. For one thing they were too interested in women (at least 80 per cent of a lower league Lad's alleged love action is shared with his fist – Lads loved the Seventies advertising slogan 'It's what your right arm's for') and not interested enough in nights out with the Lads.

For another, Lads are strictly – well, vaguely – rootsy, clinging to the wreckage of their roots even when ensconced in tax exile. Think of Rod, forlornly playing solitary football in Beverly Hills.

Lads don't invest wisely; they spend spend spend. Older Lads light cigars with £20 notes. Some Lads on the ropes have special false ones made for this purpose. A Lad loves big cars and knows the Porsche will always be with us.

Lad vocabulary is limited – 'well pissed', 'well tasty', 'legover', 'over the top', 'getting a portion', 'I don't know what came over me/got into me', 'Sorry, Mum' – but they have a rich and varied sign language life; two fingers, one finger, fist lewdly trapped in crooked elbow, grabs at each other's testicles, nudges, nods and winks. The people who write about showbiz Lads are pretty limited, too – Lads, in tabloidese, have love children, three-in-a-bed romps and Lonely Hells.

Lads don't like the cinema – all that sitting not drinking is as bad as being in church – but they like videos; *The Stud* and *The Bitch* (the heroine, Fontaine, is a Jet Set Honorary Lad herself) and especially the *Electric Blue* collections – leering at the topless Joanna Lumley when she was a poor struggling starlet rather than a luscious, pouting Lady Muck.

If they're laid up in bed, they'll read; Freddie Forsythe, *The Profession Of Violence*, Jackie Collins, rude reads in general. Lads like oral sex (getting it) and suspenders (just looking) – it makes them feel like Harold Robbins pashas, dead international.

In so far as a California valley girl can be a Lad, Joan Jett is one.

————

When young, Lads like speed with their lager and black and rum /Scotch and coke. In later, more affluent life they often go for coke proper – combining as it does fantasies of both superior sex and status – and it often plays a sizeable part in their downfall.

The current fashion for American beer makes real Lads laugh; they see it as a butch variation on wanky cocktails, started by hairdressers pushing the new short cut. (Lads do not go for the New Barberism; they are true to the dimly-lit bistro-barbers, ones that use a lot of lacquer and Roxy Music albums.)

When Lads drink, they drink to get seriously drunk, if not worse; Gary Holton died after a night's hard sauce-hitting, as did his young debby girlfriend Tracey Boyle in the late Seventies. Nigel Simmons and Mick Turton, who died of alcoholic poisoning on their Stag nights, were Lad General Custers dying with their metaphorical boots on. An honourable mention must also go to Michael Brand, who drank a cocktail of thirteen spirits mixed in a pint pot and suffered a record level of alcohol poisoning. Such is Lad.

If Lads liked poetry, they'd like 'Do not go gentle into that good night . . .' They like to think they'll burn bright and die destructively and dramatically, like Welsh poets – terrace Thomases. They like takeaways, wet T-shirt contests, women wrestling in mud and charity celebrity football – simple tastes. They get thrown out of nightclubs.

Popsies they'd like a portion of: Sam Fox, Susan George, Julie Ege.

And bits of posh: Lumley, Lenska, Vicki Hodge. (Prince Andrew is the Lad Prince.)

———

Lad Anthems: 'Maggie May', 'Stay With Me', 'The Boys Are Back In Town'.

Lads don't dance; but if they did, they'd like Cameo's 'Single Life' and Eugene Wilde's 'Gotta Get You Home' for ear-lathering reluctant blondes. Lively Lads like The Clash circa '48 Thrills', The Stranglers and Sham 69. Lads in your living room: Den and Wixey (*EastEnders*), Terry (*Minder*), Vince (*Just Good Friends*), Joey and Ray (*Fox*).

Interestingly, the boxing Fox was not a Lad – he was far too slow-witted and sensitive. Lads tend to be spindly and crafty rather than muscley, but occasionally when well tanked up they love a good scrap, they find it *cathartic*. (Lads are quite anal, and secretly enjoy the morning-after effects of excessive lager and vindaloos – with friends like that, who needs enemas?) Persistently violent people make Lads wary, though; football, once the national game, has waned with them because of the head cases and the lack of comfort. Their love of the snug has led them to snooker, poker and other card games you can play all night and act flash over. They like *Big Deal* and Hurricane Higgins. You can't drink while kicking a ball, after all.

But they do miss the communal bath afterwards; no jacuzzi ever felt so good, not even the giant-sized ones they get dunked in, if they're lucky, by American film producers' daughters in St John's Wood.

Lads are urban, but in later life, around twenty-nine when they start to look silly, they yearn for Class and the Country – meaning the Home Counties, puking distance from Stringfellows. The lucky ones are put out to grass in Surrey (showbiz) and Essex (sport) in mock Tudor houses, tended to by their Page 3 or Hot Gossip girl. They buy their parents nice bungalows; some buy stables of racehorses (Lad Stewart). They'd all like a car as long as an InterCity 125 with a bar as big as the Criterion, but Lads don't get a lot of the things they'd like these days. They've heard about Taste, poor devils, and they don't like being laughed at – especially by arty weirdos with more taste than money.

Lad has been at bay for a long time now. Officially it was punk which was supposed to get rid of *all that old tat* – pop stars who took up with thirty-five-year-old starlets, whiffed cocaine and played footsie with Princess Margaret while droning on about their working-class roots.

In reality, punk gave Lad quite a healthy booster; it was very easy for a punk to mutate into a Lad once the contract was signed, sealed and delivered. Steve Jones, Rat Scabies, Jimmy Pursey, the Hersham and Finchley Boys; Garry Bushell was the Lad Leavis, who went quite painlessly from punk to Oi to writing for the Lads' trade paper, the *Sun*.

Most youth cults, because they were essentially about male bonding, had a large element of Lad inherent in them: Teds, Rockers, Mods, Skinheads, punks, Ois. Beats weren't Lads, though, and neither were hippies. They were *girls*.

A good number of things put paid to Lad as a viable alternative for the young blood to pursue; health consciousness, herpes, tough women, being in control becoming fashionable, brasseries (Lads are strictly saloon bar), nouvelle cuisine (Lads like their nosh like Mum, *not mère*, used to make it; the only thing they love more than their girlfriend Sue is their girlfriend's suet), cocktails and other Continental crap (the only Continental thing they've got time for is French knickers, preferably on other people), Morrissey (the Anti-Lad), Mrs T (unlike their upper-middle counterparts the Hoorays, Lads hate nanny figures), men in frocks, the New Celibacy, the club scene.

But it wasn't just the big cruel world that put the kibosh on Lad. They brought a lot of it on themselves. In 1973, David Bowie released 'Aladdin Sane', and Lad was never the same again.

Something, the same indefinable thing that wiped out a generation of working-class young as TB and scarlet fever once had, about Bowie hooked them line and sinker, and they became Bowie casualties. Bowie became an alternative football team; at the concerts you could hear them with their terrace yells – 'BOOOWEE! COME ON THE BOWIE!'

There was always a streak of Latent in Lad – all that male bonding and back-combing – and Bowie brought it out.

Weirdness acted upon Lad as it had acted upon Mod in the mid-Sixties. Originally, they had looked upon all drugs but speed as 'ippie'. Now they got into them.

My husband was sent by his wealthy but mischievous father to Holloway Boys School on his arrival in this country from America. This was then a horribly tough comprehensive situated in North London. In the earliest years of the Seventies he was teased unmercifully, called hippie, a junkie and had his sushi sandwiches rubbed in his flowing locks at playtime.

In the week after 'Aladdin Sane' was released, it suddenly went all quiet on the Northern front. The bruisers began to tint their hair, wear earrings and sidle up to the poor boy in the playground; ''Ere . . . 'ippie . . . got any acid? Coke? 'Ash?' He didn't, but he was soon expelled as a vaguely drug-related 'bad influence'. I blame it on Bowie. (Like most things.)

With the self-destructiveness and lack of perspective typical of Lad, these boys attacked introspection-causing drugs with the same zeal they had once attacked alcohol and pills. Several of them went so far as to become part of the first wave of working-class junkies in Britain. But even for the rest the switch was ruinous, as it had been for Mod.

Drugs are as intrinsic a part of young lifestyles as clothes; imagine Hippie conducted on hard drinking. The last thing Mod or Lad needed was introspection, inevitably leading to self-analysis and self-doubt; they ran on the mindless, flash confidence that drink and speed only bolstered. Gary Holton had problems with heroin when he died; it is impossible to imagine, fifteen years earlier, Best or Caine or Jones – who said in a censorious Olde Lad interview in 1970, 'It takes a man to drink liquor. See, you can get high smoking pot and never get sick. But it takes a man to hold his liquor, or be able to pay the penalty' – going the same way. They would always choose Martell over marijuana.

A breed that loses faith in the stimulants that shaped it is not long for this earth; when Lad tuned in, turned on and dropped out, there were bound to be tears before bedtime.

Lads went off Bowie when he became a little soulie with 'Young Americans'; the rise of black dance music and clubs was a bodyblow to their stumbling, drunken feet and mentality. Their house bands – The Faces, Mott, Lizzy – were all dissolved by the end of the Seventies.

Despite a handful of bright spots – Stringfellows; Christopher Quentin, King Lad; Samantha Fox, the girl who rose without clothes; Paul King, a Lad pop star, all boots and boasting; the Kemp brothers, drive Porsche, play football, Lad Tendency; the Fosters ads (Oz is the last bastion of Lad rampant these days) – the Eighties have been most injurious to Lad.

Long before Holton's death, tragic Lads came to the surface; Barry Sheene's last crash (he is their Douglas Bader), Conteh's last bash (bankruptcy is very Lad), Alan Lake's last stand (his suicide was a typically extravagant Lad gesture). Jimmy Pursey came back as a *creative dancer*. Dennis Waterman (that rarity, a Jewish Lad) was tamed by his countess. Jeffrey Bernard, the reading Lad's Lad, all fags, nags and nooky, fell in love with a CND girl who bullied him. Fiona Richmond, the Muse of Lad, had a baby! – Lads are like Italians, sentimental about Mums, and couldn't look lewdly at a breast-feeding woman even if it *was* prime Richmond 36B.

Oliver Reed, that giant amongst Lads, who once said that his ideal woman was 'a deaf and dumb nymphomaniac whose father owns a chain of booze shops' – had Reed been Celtic, he might have been able to move out of Lad and over to that artisto/aristo branch, the Hell Raisers (Burton, Harris, O'Toole), who are *respected* in a way a Lad could never be – remarried after more than a decade on the rampage, at forty-seven in true Lad style to a girl of twenty-two. Even more typically, he started his stag night *two weeks before* the wedding.

But the Lad in the street was not so reliable. In a recent survey of 500 men, Smirnoff found that only 26 per cent of stag nighters had strippers or mash films while less than a third claimed their last night was in any way wild. Most of them had a *dinner party*.

Harp found that their Laddish 'Stay Sharp' adverts were becoming increasingly unpopular with their young

135

target market, and a slicker image is being sought (they sponsored the *i-D* birthday party). They've even stopped making the *Confessions* films – the Lad's James Bond.

Clutching at cocktail straws, Lads might claim George Michael as a contemporary Lad Superstar, but though 'Young Guns' was the last great Lad record, it was a *parody* record. George and Andrew are not Lads but what could be called Malteser-Smarties – too tan, too clean, too clever, too conscientiously upwardly mobile. They belong to the Club Mediterranée quietly continuing to make third-generation inroads into the Home Counties and all that implies. Malteser-Smarties have more body hair, invest their money and know when it's time to GROW UP.

Lads, alas, never do. It's a shame, because they have a real lust for life, and a spirit that many more somnambulent souls would envy. But because they have no – pardon my French – historical or economic handle on things, it all gets pissed away with the flat Castlemaine XXXX.

A mutant form of Lad, the Lad That Dare Not Speak Its Name (Gaz, Baz or Terry), lives on at the court of the boy-kings of the London club scene, those young blades whose lives, despite their boasting about having seen off Rod and Alana and all that, and despite their interest in Red Wedge – Parley Pinks, Cocaine Communists – still revolve largely around the getting of blow and blowjobs. They too will know sorrow.

Meanwhile, somewhere in that great Stringfellows in the sky, the ghost of Gary Holton is getting his leg over the ghost of Imogen Hassall, and belching with approval.

MOAN RANGERS

· · · · · · · ·

When the news came of Vaclav Havel's election to the presidency of Czechoslovakia, was I the only one to fling the shutters wide, lean out into the Dralon night and strain stock still, senses tingling, as I waited for the blasts of a hundred shotguns blaring out through every book-lined study in Hampstead, Highgate and Holland Park?

That's how you can tell they're not true gents, you see – your Pinters and Mortimers and Amises. Because any gentleman would have instinctively known that blowing one's head off was the only honourable thing to do. The Czech *kulturniks* brought down an armed police state, with both arms tied behind their backs by censorship; their British equivalent can't get one Midlands grandmother evicted, even with their books in the public lending libraries! Makes you think, eh?

Not that they haven't *talked* a good insurrection. It was Hanif Kureishi who described Eighties Britain as an authoritarian rat-hole, but it could have been any of them. Even Richard Ingrams went in for a bit of Spartspeak when he claimed Britain was a totalitarian state and compared Mrs Thatcher with Mr Ceauşescu. In the Eighties Britain's cultural dissidents really did their best

137

to behave like their Baltic brothers; they had secret meetings in huge Georgian drawing rooms and expensive Chelsea restaurants, and then wrote letters to the papers boasting about it; they issued petitions and pamphlets (see risible 'Counterblast' collection) and even had their own magazine called *Samizdat*.

Manqué see, manqué do; all they needed was a few massacres in Parliament Hill Fields and a bit of pickled herring on the breath and it would be just like Eastern Europe! – I don't think! Because, and let's get this straight, no British writer has ever known the meaning of terror. Until Salman Rushdie, that is – who then ran helter-skelter into the arms of his 'Mrs Torture' and her 'Secret Police', accepting all the machinations and subterfuge that her 'Police State' could offer in his protection. Mr Rushdie's current dependence on the trustworthiness and dedication of the police force is a piece of irony so beautiful – and such a cause for national pride and laughter – that it should hang in the Tate.

By moaning on that they were living in a country only marginally better than Stalin's Siberia, British writers no doubt believed that their colleagues in Eastern Europe would take this as a mark of respect and fellowship. Would you or I, though, I wonder? If we were having our noses pulled off and our eyes gouged out by some *Securitate* bastard, and the cry went up from beside a hundred swimming pools in Tuscany, 'Our thoughts are with you, brother – because *we* live in a totalitarian state too!' – would you feel well-chuffed that Harold and Antonia were having a nice chat about you over their Earl Grey, and that they could really, really empathize? I don't think I would; I think I'd want to pull their noses off and gouge their eyes out. Nothing personal, mind you.

In the Eighties, totalitarian regimes became, for certain sensitive men, what Porsches are for the coarser creatures – penis extensions, which make them feel young and lusty and outrageous again. You could understand them, and that their feeling was genuine rather than staged made it in a way all the more pathetic. In the Seventies, with Labour smug as a bug in a rug, your Mortimers and Pinters had been on the safe side, the *in* side, but with the election of Mrs Thatcher, male menopause became second childhood; the middle-aged spread, the burst veins and the nose fungus disappeared – though the nice houses didn't, fortunately – and they were angry young bloods again, fighting the Fascisti down the Ridley Road!

You could see why it was so irresistible to the sort of man who'd started out thirty years ago with righteous fire in his belly – and now was left with little more than heartburn from the rich sauces his third wife liked to practise on him, and whose sole contribution towards wealth distribution in the Seventies was Bob-A-Job week. Mrs Thatcher may have been a wet liberal's worst enemy, but she was also his wettest dream – she made him feel young, an outlaw and a real Lefty again, even though he was old and fat and rich and ugly. She gave him back his balls.

Salman Rushdie, writing in *Granta*, sounded the call to the word processor. 'If writers leave the business of making pictures of the world to politicians, it will be history's greatest and most abject abdication.' Films (*The Ploughman's Lunch*, *My Beautiful Launderette*, *Paris By Night*), plays (*The Secret Rapture*, *Serious Money*), novels galore, petitions and polemics rained down upon the nation like a tickertape parade. 'There is a need,' said Rushdie, 'for political fiction, for books that draw new and better maps of reality.' Wipe my nose and call me snotty, but 'drawing a new map of reality' sounds like Ponceyspeak for *lying* to me.

The problem was that the new map of Thatcher's Britain looked very much like the map of Wilson, Heath and Callaghan's Britain, when you looked closely – racist, snobbish, greedy and dead cold, not like Tuscany. In the novels of Margaret Drabble and Martin Amis, their descriptions of Eighties Britain sound *exactly* like their descriptions of Seventies Britain! Which in turn sound like both Sixties Britain (*Cathy Come Home*) and Fifties Britain (*Look Back In Anger*), and a lot, come to think of it, like Forties Britain (*Hangover Square*). If you took the trouble, I bet you could go back and find some moping member of the Iceni tribe wearing Hush Puppies and a Paul Foot haircut and moaning on about Boudica's Britain.

But if all these awful things started with Mrs Thatcher, how can this be so? Someone must be telling a whopper. And writers being what they are – people *paid* for making things up – you don't have to be V.I. Warshawski to find out who.

It is only when reading the novels of Margaret Drabble that I have any sympathy for people who lash out and cut down a spouse who has been nagging at them ceaselessly for forty years. Says the heroine of her latest flop *A Natural Curiosity*, 'England's not a bad country – it's just a mean, cold, ugly, divided, tired, clapped-out, post-imperial, post-industrial slag heap covered in polystyrene hamburger cartons.' Fair enough; myself, I like it that way – and this view comes much closer, incidentally, towards drawing a new map of reality than the pre-Raphaelite dream of pre-industrial bliss that Drabble dribbles on about. But the point is that this tirade could just as easily have come from her Seventies novel *The Ice Age* – when Labour were in power, her books were on the chart, her husband lived at home and all was presumably right with the world.

Suppose the greenhouse effect happens and England gets as warm as Tuscany, and suppose we all go Green and don't drop rubbish – what the Sam Hill is this old broad going to do for a living when she can't write crap books about how cold, dirty and horrid England is any more? No wonder her husband lives on the other side of town, if her table talk in any way resembles her writing.

Yes, in that fictional dystopia called Thatcher's Britain, the streets are paved with polystyrene while lager louts lurk in a fog of violence. But the novelist's accuracy as reporter, and the purity of his moral anguish, is compromised something rotten by his amnesia concerning Britain *before* the beast. Only Bob Geldof characteristically broke ranks when he said: 'I hated the Seventies – they were mean and nasty. They talk about selfishness in the Eighties, but I've never seen anything like *that* period.' It takes a big man to admit that things were worse in the past, and that he is not the bravest person of all time. For the moral pygmies of Thatcher-bashing, such an admission would cause an implosion of self-worth and self-regard comparable to suicide; they just cannot risk it. So they forget, and they pretend.

In the post-modern morass of moral relativism, the stereotypes (Yuppie bastards) and simple equations (aspiration equals greed) of Thatcher's Britain provide a comforting certainty. From living in a land composed of shades of grey, liberals now have a simple black and white world – like the one she promised *her* people. Old Testament rantings on greed and hedonism no longer come from the Right, but from such as Jeanette Winterson writing in the *New Statesman*: 'Cecil Parkinson's very existence depends on a society to whom standards of behaviour no longer matter. He has proved that not only do we fail to punish people who behave appallingly, but we reward them.' For God's sake, all the smarmy git did was commit adultery! – is she suggesting we stone him to death outside the city walls? What is this? Some bizarre form of lesbian Islam?

Even a sharpie like Hanif Kureishi will claim that he feels himself to be part of a pre-Thatcher England of tolerance and decency; stone me, what happened to the sins of Suez and the endemic racism of Little England, amongst others? An England where, Mortimer says – before the Tory Party was taken 'down market' – 'the local squire would hand out tea and tins of biscuits at Christmas.' He does not say whether the peasants tugged their forelocks in gratitude; but never mind, such old-world chivalry would surely have brought tears to the eyes of this good radical.

Ultimately, the failure of the 'serious' writer was his sacrifice of that one thing he had prided himself on above all: the artist's commitment to the truth. Never once in all the plays and polemic did any anti-Thatcher writer hint that there lurked within himself or his audience any germ of a longing for status or wealth. And all those Right-On NT audiences could leave the Lyttelton safe and secure in the knowledge that they, untainted by Thatcherism, could walk across the water to the Savoy bar.

But don't tell me that Steven Berkoff's Dockland penthouse or Stephen Fry's fleet of sports cars are some sort of puckish, ironic, anti-materialistic jape. Don't tell me that Rushdie and Weldon dumped the publishers who had nursed and nourished them when offered serious money by big conglomerates in the name of art. Personally, I don't blame them – *I* never met a massive advance I didn't like, either. But then I don't go around slagging off other people as greedy Thatcherite bastards if they want a nice big bite of life or a second home in Chiantishire. And when the Pinters announced their departure from their June 20 group – that very epicentre of dissident England – due to the 'burden of work' (which roughly translates as 'our brilliant careers'), you had to laugh.

The modern writer is not the conscience of his times, but a tourist in them, an Awayday dissident who, on arriving at the last junction of youth, turns back and heads for home, Queen and country. Comrade Spencer becomes a Sir; angry Osborne a born-again Blimp. In retrospect, how ridiculous the ranting writer appears: 'Damn you, England – you're rotting now and quite soon you will disappear. My hate will outrun you,' said Osborne in 1961. Your average end-of-the-pier Madame Rosa has a better prophecy rate than your average British writer.

Whether it's Rushdie, for whom the police state is now a life-support machine, or Amis announcing that we're all about to die ten minutes before the Cold War ends, so much for the serious writer's special antenna! And so much for the *truth*. With his references to Mrs Torture, Rushdie's other offence was not to the British people, as Geoffrey Howe said (we can take it; we can take *anything*), but to language itself. Because if Thatcher is a torturer, what do you call Pinochet? When it comes to shameless mutilation of language, and the twisting of the truth, Rushdie is right up there with the big league liars – Ceauşescu, Kissinger and Khomeini.

As for you, Amis Minor (*very* minor) – get back to writing about armpits, toe jam and bachelor pads while there's still time, why don't you? Do yourself a favour – leave the Big Issues to us Gentlemen of the Press. You know it makes sense.

BABY BOOM

· · · · · · · ·

Suddenly everyone is going gaga – and goo-goo – over things that go 'WAAAAAH!' in the night. The Duchess of York is eating for two (instead of for five, as she was previously), the fertile-at-forty lobby smirk smugly over designer bulges from the pages of glossy magazines and American screen actors have given up mumbling and riding motorcycles in favour of making a meal out of changing a nappy. Post-AIDS, the cinema has swopped soft-focus adult nudity (dangerous) for full-frontal baby nudity (safe); from being the little devils of the Seventies – *Demon Seed*, the *Damian* trilogy – they have become the little darlings of the Eighties – *Baby Boom*, *Three Men And A Baby*, *She's Having A Baby*, *Raising Arizona*, *For Keeps*.

These films, of course, are invariably written by the childless, by men or by women with babyminders. As usual, the wonders of having children are shouted about the loudest by those who do it the least. Those who can, never do; those who do don't write screenplays about the wonder of babies because they're too exhausted at the end of the day to put hand to mouth, let alone pen to paper.

145

Even *lesbians*, these days, want babies. This to me is particularly appalling, though not for any bogus moral reason; judging from the statistics, a child with two mothers is less likely to be raped by a parent than a child with a 'normal' mother and father. No, I find it appalling because surely the best thing about being a lesbian is the glorious freedom from the whole kit and caboodle of horrible heterosex side effects of the kind that afflict and kill women in their thousands every year – VD, cervical cancer, thrombosis from the Pill, stretch marks, abortion. That lesbians are now voluntarily taking on the most lethal side effect of heterosexuality of all, *pregnancy*, convinces me that homosexuals are more than a little mad.

This new sentimentality sees children as the embodiment of innocence, untainted by the corruption of the adult world. Picasso – in what must surely have been his Blind Period – even said that all children were artists.

Nonsense. People talk about the greed and selfishness of Eighties Britain, but when it comes to these qualities children since time immemorial have been the ankle-biting shock-troops of Thatcherism, inhabiting a world where self-interest and rampant consumerism rule the roost. Any civilizing compassion society might have is due solely to the influence of innocent and artistic adults.

Crazy eco-feminists and equally crazy anti-feminists have seen to it that your average baby is little less than a jailer who could more than hold his own rattling the keys at Strangeways. From 'enjoying' the pain of labour, to letting the baby sleep in the bed for the first three years, to not getting a job until Baby reaches the age of twenty-one; that way lies madness, divorce and very little nooky.

To the maternity mafia, any woman who wants to go to a restaurant without her baby is guilty of child abuse. There is a certain sort of berk who is forever saying, 'Oh, in England we *hate* children – whereas in France and Italy, they're welcomed into pubs and cafés and everything! And no one minds!'

This is not true. I mind. And I know many other people, men and women, parents or not, who mind a great deal. Having taken the trouble to arrange a babysitter for your own brat, one does not wish to go out to enjoy the sophisticated company of other adults only to have the ambience shattered by a bawling baby. If you wanted that, you'd hang around a nursery school, not go out to a bar.

Few things are as unconducive to a romantic dinner *à deux* than the pungent waft of a nappy being changed. Unless it is the sight of a baby being fed from a breast resembling a punctured barrage balloon. Public breast-feeding is a disgusting habit, and one no better than flashing. If I ever see it, I shall call the police and complain of public indecency. Objections are countered with the moronic cliché that such a practice is 'only natural'. But so are the elimination process and the sexual act, and if we did those in public we would quite rightly be arrested.

By keeping children with us we not only spoil the fun of other adults, but theirs too. I remember numerous idyllic summer evenings when I and my friends got up to all kinds of no good in the fields around the rural pubs that banned our presence while our parents drank themselves insensible, coming out once in a while to throw us yet another bag of Smiths crisps and a bottle of Tizer. It was heavenly. There is nothing a child likes less than having an 'eye' kept on it constantly, as is common practice in those wretched killjoy Continental pubs.

In the current crop of films, bringing up baby is portrayed as an experience which humanizes people. But it doesn't – it *dehumanizes*. As we are always being told, human nature is competitive, aggressive and selfish – that's why we've had Mrs Thatcher reigning over us for the last nine years. To look after a baby properly you have to be non-competitive, passive and altruistic – that is, you have to de-construct your human nature. *Someone* has to do it, like coal-mining, but it's not very good for your health. The proof is in the pudding in our monetarist society; no one who can afford not to look after their own children does it, with very few exceptions, for more than a year. Those who *are* forced by circumstances to go against their human nature suffer greatly.

A conference of the Royal College of Physicians recently unveiled a study showing that mothers were three times more likely than other women to suffer from depression. Dr Paul Bebbington of the London Institute of Psychiatry said, 'Having children renders you susceptible to depression for the rest of your life.' And who is to say that the modern epidemics of incest and male homosexuality do not owe something to the equally modern habit of smothering children with the sort of incessant and intimate physical contact that might be better reserved for appetizing and consenting fellow adults?

The rich and the poor, until this century, never placed too much importance on who brought their babies up. The rich farmed them out to the poor and the poor farmed them out to their own extended families, those too young or old to work. Bringing up your own baby is as modern and lower-middle class as net curtains, and just as aesthetically attractive.

The Victorians maintained the strictest division between the worlds of adults and children that this country has ever seen. Half an hour at tea time; another after bathing and before bed. This left the Victorians lots of time for the important things of adult life, such as building empires and indulging in kinky sexual practices. For the good of ourselves and our children, let this be one Victorian value we truly take to our hearts.

POSTURES GREEN

. . . .

So familiar did the scenario for life as she will be lived in the Nice Age Nineties become during the last year of the Eighties that outbreaks of ennui, and of nostalgia for the sexy-greedy designer decade itself, broke out even before the Nineties had got its hessian sandal off the starting block.

At the height of Nineticipation, the media still churned out a ceaseless stream of Eighties icons: the ecstatic young brokers crouched over their computer screens as if about to paint their masterpieces – 'GILLETTE! THE BEST A MAN CAN GET!' – the power-pouted career girls coming on hot and strong over cups of ersatz coffee, and both of them battling it out from bedroom to boardroom and back again in prime-time dramas.

You can say what you like about the Eighties (and you do; just like the Yuppie, the decade's folk demon who inspired a wave of moral panic not amongst the Disgusteds of Tunbridge Wells but amongst the Horrifieds of Hampstead, the Eighties per se has become a useful whipping boy for externalizing and condemning all the qualities we dislike in ourselves – God knows what we will blame our lust, greed and materialism on in the

Nineties, or after Margaret) but it was definitely the best-dressed decade so far. And this was because sartorially, if in no other way, the Eighties reverted to classical values; not since the Thirties had so many women worn red lipstick, high heels and shoulder pads, or so many men worn suits. One of the most attractive features of the Eighties, exemplified by its chosen drag, was its willingness to *make an effort*.

This year's collections saw a swing away from power-dressing – and the rag trade fag hags looked upon it, and said it was good. But are we sure about this? Isn't the opposite of power-dressing power*less*-dressing? The new vision of woman coming down the catwalks of Europe's capitals is not, as some pundits have claimed, a liberation – but a capitulation.

Women in white wearing sandals and carrying babies – Laura Ashley meets the Maharishi. The tough women in jersey dresses who slunk through the wet dreams and nightmares of Eighties Man have been replaced by these castrates in cashmere, these svelte Earth Mothers who look like refugees from an OMO WASHES WHITER casting call; from cracking the whip to will o' the wisp. Not fun, not sexy (New Age is the first cult to be instigated by the middle-aged rather than the young, a reflection of the approaching demographical shift away from teenagers; put the menopause and AIDS together with the middle-aged spread of the mind and the fear of modernity that comes with the ageing process, and the essential *cowardliness* of New Ageism – which might better be called Old Ageism – becomes clear) and certainly not practical; I bet those white Ozbek djellabahs didn't look half so ethereal after those designer babies had finished chucking up their organic muesli all over those models, heh heh.

The collections illustrated very nicely a paradox which, so far, the growing hordes of Green Moderns have chosen not to confront. And that is this: *how can the popular culture of the post-war West, which we have loved and lived for, drawn strength from and consoled ourselves with, live alongside the New Age mentality?*

There are many reasons to distrust and despise Greenism; its misanthropy (Greens seem to hear the screams of Latin American rainforests being chopped down, but not the screams of Latin American people being tortured for the sin of trying to form trades unions), its naivety (Mother Nature as a caring, sharing Sheila Kitzinger type rather than the earthquake-throwing, starvation-causing celestial lager lout on a permanent bender she so obviously is) and its privileged stupidity ('Quality of life' vs materialism indeed! – only someone who had never been poor would think it possible to have a good quality of life without a lot of money). But its probable effect on popular culture is the reason to be fearful I shall pursue here.

It is ironic that so many of those currently embracing the New Age of Green (or NAG, as I'll call it – for the sake of convenience, and to get up your nose) are the same types who drone on about the 'Philistinism' of Thatcherism being such a threat to this country's culture. Well, I've got news for them. In the Nineties, the threat to modern culture will come not from the low-minded Tories – but from the high-minded Greens.

For this reason, as many NAG politicos have been keen to point out; going Green doesn't end with saving this or re-cycling that. It demands, in the name of survival, a radical change in sensibility, values and Self. It sees the modern Western Self, with its estrangement from Nature, its egotism and its pursuit of excess, as essentially *sick*, and in danger of infecting the whole planet with this fatal distraction. To remedy this, NAG proposes a self that is in tune with Nature – an organic whole. (Or an organic *hole*, in the case of women – whose entire history and legacy of emancipation is based on fighting tooth and claw against Mother Nature and her diktats. Girls *never* agree with their mothers, and we shouldn't make an exception for this bossy old broad.) But who the hell wants to be a healthy organic whole when you can be a brilliant, injured, human fragment?

NAG is poised to be the Freudianism of the twenty-first century; it wants to *cure* the patient, making him holistic, harmonious, happy – in other words, *well-adjusted*. And like Freud, NAG is a deeply reactionary and insensitive dogmatist, when you get right down to it; why should a single mother in a bed and breakfast hovel or a crack-addicted black man feel kindly towards the planet that gave them such lousy lives? Hence the decrease in Green adherents as one goes down the social scale, and the suspicious interest of the super-rich in environmental issues. Of course they're interested in keeping the planet nice; they hold the property rights.

NAG seeks to give the modern world a spiritual enema, cleansing the polluted cesspool of the Western psyche until it stands shiny and new, rising like Venus from her conch. Yet it is from that very cesspool that strange and wonderful things crawl; great modern art is born from the collision of the outer and inner worlds, not the reconciliation. Freud wanted to adjust man to the bourgeois order of *fin-de-siècle* Vienna; the Greens want to adjust him to the whole bleeding universe.

But look! – what's this in front of me? Why, it's the

bran tub of twentieth-century culture! I'm putting in my hot little hand – and I've pulled out Marilyn Monroe, Jim Morrison, Sylvia Plath and Marvin Gaye! But it could have been a million other of those people – you know, those people we grew up wanting to be, fuck, die for – and they'd still have all these things in common, *our heroes*. None of them would be in harmony with the universe and all of them would be neurotic, narcissistic, ambitious, self-loathing and self-destructive – but nobody's perfect! They were also pretty *nice*. Yes, boys and girls, it can be done.

And I love them all. This – not Shakespeare, not Stonehenge – is *my* culture; the international fraternity of Neurotic Boy and Girl Outsiders. Our very culture has been created by a monstrous regiment of drunks, egomaniacs, sadists, masochists, dope fiends, self-adoring faggots, self-disgusted heteros – and I wouldn't have it any other way. Just imagine if Saint Marilyn had been a centred and harmonious person! – why, she would have wound up making cakes like Jane Asher or being an all-round wonderful poisson like Joanna Lumley! Which is *surely* a fate worse than death. It is the very imperfection of the *person* that makes the perfect icon.

Our modern culture is based in the City; not the NAG city of stable communities, clean streets, smokeless zones and carnivals, but the city of skyscrapers and sleaze, of girls called Lois working for great metropolitan newspapers, of sad and clever drunks sitting around round tables, of men who are not themselves mean having to go down these mean (not clean, not Green) streets.

One of this century's outstanding works of art is Jim Morrison's 'L.A. Woman'; it is interesting to imagine what would be left of this great song had it passed through the NAG blender. Just take one stanza:

> Cops in cars,
> The topless bars,
> Never saw a woman
> So alone.

Which translates into Ecospeak as:

> Active citizens on bikes,
> The fruit juice bars,
> Never saw a person
> So much in their own space.

Get the picture? Not many, Benny!

Imagine, if you please, what a New Age *film noir* would be like! – when those James Cain bitches got bored with their husbands, they wouldn't recruit some hunky drifter to kill him; they'd go to Relate! Imagine if 'Nighthawks' had been painted by a New Ager – they'd all be sitting outside in the sunshine, sipping camomile tea, smiling like there was a tomorrow! If New Age had been holding the wheel that steered the twentieth century, we would have had no jazz (created by dope fiends), no Hollywood glamour girls (sexist), no Americana (wasteful, ethnocentric), no Madonna (materialistic), NO IMMAC!!!

We need only look back at the morning after the Sixties to see the rubbish that passes for culture in an age of Eco-Doom; Paul and Linda, Shirley MacLaine, Jonathan Livingstone Seagull, Woodstock, ponchos, mood rings, ankhs and posters proclaiming you to be a child of the frigging universe, if you please. *Nothing black, nothing sexy, nothing sleazy? – nothing doing!* might well be the motto of modern culture.

NAG seeks to make us feel good about ourselves. But what's so good about feeling good about oneself? Isn't that about as smug, complacent and Me Generationish as it gets? Maybe us *not* feeling good about ourselves is what took us so far; made us the only culture in the world where life is not a toss up between horror and boredom.

To reiterate, I do not wish to be part of an organic whole, thank you very much, and anyone who tries to coerce me will get a fat lip. Furthermore, in a fit of pure childish pique, every time I see Sara Parkin or Jonathon Porritt telling me what's best for me, I'm going to grab an aerosol and not even *pretend* to spray under my arms, I'M GOING TO LEAN OUT THE WINDOW AND AIM IT STRAIGHT AT THE OZONE LAYER! (The ozone layer has become the Queen Mother of Spaceship Earth.) And like all brilliant, flawed babes – and New Age is nothing if not the revenge of the dull upon the brilliant – I'd rather pull myself apart than get myself together. To paraphrase the Elephant Man: I AM NOT A HUMAN BEING – I AM A FREAK!

Anyone tempted to go Green; just do this one thing for me, will you? Take some fast drugs and read Marinetti while listening to 'I Am What I Am', LOUD. Then do this: sip some Aqua Libre while listening to Peruvian nose flute music and reading the Desiderata. Done it? Right? GOTCHA!

In saving ourselves, we will kill the thing we love. Please. Just for me. For Marilyn, for Jim, for Marvin. Just say no.

MY BEST FRIEND'S NOVEL OR
WHAT YOUR BEST FRIEND WON'T TELL YOU

. . . .

When I was a little girl, there was a famous television commercial for deodorant – unusually frank for its day, looking back. Two men in suits – one serenely unself-conscious, the other doing a good impersonation of Martin Amis (smell under nose, world on shoulders) – stand side by side. Finally, the troubled one leans close to the happy one and whispers 'B.O.!' The voice-over booms 'B.O. – what your best friend can't tell you!'

These days, everyone over the age of eight is familiar with deodorants, so this really isn't a modern problem. But every friendship still faces the moment of no return. For Andy Warhol, the beginning of the end of a new friendship came when the P.L.O. (Potential Loved One) started calling up at three in the morning; these 'insecure' people would suddenly find that their fifteen minutes was up. A big hurdle is when your friend falls in love, and brings the new kid by for a once-over; what do you say if you fervently believe that he's a dog/she's a pig? The best bet is to lie, wait till they bust up and *then* tell the truth – 'I never liked them, anyway.' Putting the truth on hold, so to speak. Personally, I've had friendships which have survived the psychosis of drink, the delirium of drugs and the horrors of the doldrums – but there is one thing, one question that no friendship can survive. Just seven little words: 'What did you think of my novel?'

Until very recently, such questions were not asked in mixed company. Such reticence was not due to innate good manners, but to the fact that until the mid-Eighties, hipsters were not *writing* novels. The literate ones wanted to be hacks; the novel was considered to be an archaic form, labour intensive, over-manned, with a low financial return – dead meat. We'd all read Tom Wolfe's bit in the *New Journalism* where he boasted that the 'new' journalist had replaced the novelist as the chronicler of the age. Wolfe's cubs wanted it now – easy money and quick fame. So they locked themselves away in the Limelight StarBar and got down to some serious drinking – 'collecting material', we used to call it.

So all was well until the appearance of Jay Brett Janowitz and the gang. The beast we'd believed was buried beneath the floorboards of Foyle's with a stake driven through its heart – the novel – was back, smirking out self-adoringly from the Style pages of the Sunday supplements; the pages where we'd grown so used to reading about the antics of our friends (i.e. other hacks). Suddenly it wasn't enough to write a thousand words about nightclubs; now you had to write fifty thousand words about nightclubs to get any air time. And then you had a *novella*, for Frig's sake! A novel would take till *Christmas*. (Christmas in *Iran*.)

The Great London Novel became the Loch Ness Monster of literary London. There were false sightings every couple of months, but no one could prove its existence. And knowing they were thus in with a chance, all the hacks came out of the stationery closet and admitted that all the time they'd been practising to be Peter York, they'd really wanted to be Martin Amis! (It was easier, for one thing.) And when the news spread that TOM WOLFE – the man who'd written the novel off! – had actually *written the novel* . . . well, that was it. The novel was back in favour and fashion before you could say 'remaindered'.

Of course, for a year or two it was a phoney war of words; one's friends *talked* about a good novel, though rather like suicide you could bet your bottom credit card that those who talked about it would never actually have the nerve to go ahead and do the thing. But as the school-teacher who always got saddled with the school trip used to say, there's always *one* who has to spoil it for everyone else. And so a couple of indecently indelicate individuals actually went out of their way to finish their books. And not content with flouting the boundaries of decency, some even went so far as to have them published.

Suddenly, babies and novels are everywhere; the essential holsters of the hip young gunslinger. Novels are actually very similar to babies – with conception comes throwing up in the mornings, and with completion comes sleepless nights. And, I fear, like their babies, your friends' novels should be seen but never heard from.

In theory, it's a breeze, Louise. In theory, when presented with a friend's novel, you should be both touched and flattered; your altruism and narcissism chemicals should go on red alert, ready to gush like Jett Rink's black gold. It is an advanced form of both social and creative bonding, like being asked to be best man at his wedding by the man who's presenting you with the Booker Prize. It says both I TRUST YOU and YOU'RE SPECIAL. On paper, this is an irresistible combo.

But on paper signed with a name from your little black book, this is a different proposition. Into your hands it comes, bless its little forked tongue, in unreadable manuscript or panting proof (I've always thought that 'proof' copies of books were so called because here at last is the proof you've always wanted that X can't write for shit), with that little personal dedication tucked away like a bribe. You are curious, and like a good intellectual give the jacket photo a quick dekko. Mmm – shares in Cheesebrough-Pond's must have *shot* up the day they took this one, judging from the amount of Vaseline they put on the lens. Especially when you take into consideration that X's complexion makes the Rocky Mountains look like chiffon velvet most days of the month. MIAOW!

You have a good snigger at the blurb ('Provocative, perverse and shocking' – X's ex says that too, albeit referring to a technique slightly more personal than their writing) and put it away, saving it, like a treat – or like Maths homework. You say to yourself, if it's bad, I'll be upset for X; if it's good, I'll be upset for me. Then you realize that either way – Booker or bull – you can't lose. If it is really good, then you have an incredibly talented and famous writer as your friend; if it's crap, then you have the deep, warm glow – like taking brandy intravenously – of knowing that you are still the most incredibly talented and famous writer your friends know.

So you turn to page one. Uh-oh – one of those creative punctuation jobs. Fasten your seatbelt, black coffee, lots of it – there's a crazy on the plane, and nowhere to land. Page three arrives on schedule and you toy with the concept of doing a little light dusting. Page five, and the narrator has switched to third person, and another century, is turning into a sausage (pork) and – oh my

Gawd, here comes twenty pages of a dream they had twenty years ago at primary school!

For the next couple of weeks, you live in fear and incognito. You don't answer the phone or the intercom except in a strangulated Bratislavian accent – 'Yass? Iss no here. Iss gone away.' You wake up your better half in the middle of the night so you can polish your responses. You've come up with three that you think are pretty good:

'It's very commercial!' – *It's trash*.

'Parts of it really worked!' – *It stank*.

'It's the first truly post-modern novel' – *It's trash and it stank*.

But a month passes, and it looks like you're in the clear. Surely they wouldn't ask *now* – that would make it a pre-meditated crime, as opposed to a *crime passionel*. That would make it *cold-blooded*. So when they call up one night – the lateness of the hour is a good warning sign; they're having insecure thoughts – you're a little apprehensive. But what the hell – if you don't mention it, there's no way they will. No one's got that much front.

You dish the dirt, make a date to make a date, and the shore is in sight – you're actually grinning manically at your husband and making the high sign with your free hand – when they strike.

'By the way – what did you think of my novel?'

As the scream dies on your lips, every bad review you've ever got flashes before your eyes.

There are two ways, at the end of the day, to handle the situation – tell a little lie, or tell a big lie. One thing is sure: no one will thank you for telling the truth. In our mind's eye, the hack pack like to picture themselves as a hybrid of Oscar Wilde and Albert Schweitzer; we like to think we will listen to criticism with humility and forbearance, head bowed, nodding occasionally, before coming back, unbeaten, with a riposte that is both generous-spirited and wickedly stinging; which slyly puts the finger on the critic while showing him there's no hard feelings.

In reality, we are more likely to scowl, burst into tears and snatch said dedicated proof back with a shrill 'Please, let me take this off your hands!' before running off to sulk, brood and eventually pay them back in some horribly childish ways so low that they are not even worth mentioning. But a particular favourite of mine, when *Ambition* was doing the rounds and on the ropes, was to send off applications to computer dating agencies in the critic's name, taking care to request correspondents from all the dullest and most unattractive categories. There may be worse things than being inundated with mash letters from sixty-year-old Catholics fond of gardening and embroidery, but I haven't thought of one yet.

Like swopping wives or lending records, speaking the phrase 'Tell me honestly what you think' is a mortal blow from which a friendship never fully recovers. And, just like the first two activities, it always seems such a good idea at the time. After a good nosh, a bottle or three of Stoly, with the lights down low and Brook Benton on the radio, what could be better than a little light honesty? The answer is – most things, including a strangulated hernia.

So I myself would never dream these days of asking a friend what they thought of me; the line 'if you can't say something nice, say nothing' has never yet been bettered when it comes to the near and dear novel. Those who just can't help themselves – well, they get what's coming to them. Of all my novelist friends, a man called Caris Davis has set the best example to us all; when his – actually very good – book *Stealth* saw the light of day, he packed his bags and dragged his wife seven thousand miles over land and sea to a small shack – without telephone – in the middle of the mid-West of the USA. That was six months ago, and they're still there. As the literary equivalent of going into the library to shoot yourself through the head – as Victorian cads were wont to do upon seeing the desirability of doing the decent thing – that takes some beating.

THE PATHOLOGY OF PLEASURE

· · · · · · · ·

They used to say that the road of excess led to the palace of wisdom; not in the Eighties it didn't. In the Eighties, it led to Kilroy, Kitzinger and Claire Rayner; to the cathode confessional and the privatized problem lines of British Telecom. In the Eighties, the road of excess led to the palazzo of pathologization.

A funny thing happened on the way to the millennium; suddenly, everything that had previously been thought of as a pleasure turned out to be a problem. Because pleasurable activities are pleasurable, it is only natural that we tend to repeat them as often as we can; in the Eighties, this normal human response suddenly became known as addiction. And it turned out you could be addicted to practically anything: food, shopping, spending, sex, love and Space Invaders. And there was I thinking people did them just for cheap thrills! That was the thing about the Eighties; you didn't do things for kicks, but because you were sick.

How did it happen and where did it come from? It is, I believe, a Puritan response filtered through the socio-speak of the caring professions. Value judgements are avoided like the plague these days; therefore we couldn't call behaviour *bad*. But we could say that it was bad *for* one. By turning vices into viruses, we avoid the problem of – heaven forbid! – passing judgement.

This is fine for the caring professional pundits, who can dispense doomy prophecies and cheery advice until the cows come home without ever having to put their necks on the line and say that one way of living is better than another. But the pathologization of pleasure has in many ways made Eighties Britain a more morose and moribund place for the rest of us.

'Mustn't grumble' – once our national caricature catchphrase – has become '*Must* grumble, preferably on Yoof TV.' Once upon a time, teenagers were golden creatures who had more sex and took more drugs and dreamed more dreams than anybody else, envied by all for their beauty, nerve and daring. Not any more; you turn on the TV, and see some teenager staring sullenly out at you, and you KNOW what he's there for – he's there to complain. About the drugs he does, the computer games he plays, the life he leads – anything will do. The cult of Miserabilism – patron saint Morrissey – has brainwashed British youth to a depressing degree.

When I was a teenager in the late Seventies – and one inevitably ends up sounding like some crusty old colonel when one tries this 'In my day . . .' tack, but it can't be helped – my friends and I took it for granted that one lived in a septic squat or dossed down on assorted floors, had no money to speak of (as a cub reporter I was paid so little that I had to return deposit bottles to shops to get the bus fare to work) and spent what little one had on a numbing combo of sulphate and snakebite, which took you right out of your box and left you with a hangover *and* hallucinations (apparently amphetamine turns to mescalin after thirty-six hours use without food). Maybe we were naive, but none of us – poor, drug-taking, living in squalor – thought we had a *problem*; we were having *fun*. The most unattractive thing about young people today is that they do not glory in their excesses, but regard them as a problem that some politician should solve.

Two groups have dissented from the Miserabilist Tendency of the Eighties, and both have been roundly reviled. There are the Acid Housers, who are basically little more than the heirs of Mod – dancers on drugs, living for the weekend, very unlikely to pose any sort of threat to straight society (like the Mods, a surprising number of Acid Housers work as bank tellers).

But the media's attitude to Acid House youth, as opposed to junkies, is revealing. A junkie welches from the state, discards syringes in public places and spreads AIDS. Yet he is the recipient of nothing but sympathy. Acid House kids are regarded with hostility and fear – because of their very refusal to conform to society's stereotype of the drug abuser. They have jobs, money and fun; they are, in some ways, an advertisement for recreational drugs, or at least proof that drugs can be assimilated into an ordinary, successful, enjoyable life. The junkie is everyone's favourite victim because he conforms to society's view of the drug user; he's a mess. His excesses have brought him not fun but pain; he has a *problem*, therefore he can be forgiven. Sure the Acid Housers wear clothes that would get them shot in any just society; but their refusal to equate excess with misery and ruin is admirable.

Then there are the Big Bang Boys (which itself sounds like a Malcolm McLaren dream concept destined never to leave the drawing board – *that* perfect). These boys were a hippie's nightmare; they too believed in sex, drugs, fast cars and rock and roll (albeit on CD) – AND THEY WERE FLAMING CAPITALISTS! A perfect synthesis of straight ambition and counterculture hedonism – it has been claimed that 80 per cent of London's cocaine users work in the City – naturally they appalled both sides. But their easy mating of hell-raising and hard work – their refusal to see drink and drugs as problems, but as the icing on the cake of conspicuous consumption – was an inspiration to us all. In an age when a pop star's idea of a good time is a glass of Badoit and a benefit concert, the Big Bang Boys were the wild boys of the Eighties; Rolling Stones in Rolexes.

The Eighties was the decade in which Mary Tyler Moore sought treatment for alcoholism because, each evening on returning home from work, she drank two martinis. TWO. Until the Eighties, two martinis after work was called unwinding. Now it's called alcoholism. We may yet find that this habit of seeing a problem behind every pleasure was the stupidest and most morally enervating of all Eighties excesses.

NOW IS THE TIME FOR ALL GOOD MEN
TO COME TO THE AIDS PARTY

. . . .

There are many interesting parallels between Madonna – Madame Mercury, Femme Of A Thousand Faces, the T-1000 of pop – and our own dear Princess of Wales. Both were motherless children from boring backwaters – Bay City, Michigan and Althorp House, Northampton. Both were voluptuous brunettes who became skinny blondes. Both are regular little party animals, saying no to drink, drugs, smoking and meat, and exercising like things possessed. Both have big noses; both are good dancers; both married incredibly ugly men. Both were wise virgins, losing their virginity only as a 'career move', as the bolder of the frat-pack put it. And both, it seems, have a high regard for homosexual men, usually found in women suffering from some sexual dysfunction. Together, they have become the only really first-rate patrons of the AIDS Brigade.

Not a month goes by without Madonna receiving a citation from the AIDS lobby for her outspoken views on safe sex and the paintings of Keith Haring, which she has been courageous enough to admit she admires. And here, let a homosexual only stub his toe and he will come to to find the Princess snivelling beside his bed as if her heart would break. Previously regarded with great suspicion by the Right-Ons – for their fervent interest in money and clothes – they are now both beyond reproach. And no wonder. For without them, the AIDS bandwagon would be revealed – morally, aesthetically and commercially – as the old banger it is.

Up to 15 million children in the Third World, mostly in sub-Saharan Africa, will lose their mothers to AIDS by the end of the century. The developing countries contain 75 per cent of the world's AIDS infection; by the year 2000 they will have more than 90 per cent. Yet, shamefully, and with the connivance of the AIDS charities, the disease is now being treated as a cross between a Neighbourhood Watch scheme and an excuse for a knees-up. While whole African villages are wiped out by this plague, the Western media continue to regale us with a shock-horror roll-call of a generation of creative genius (without exception male and Euro/American) lost forever.

This sounds pretty impressive until you inspect the faces close up; not the pillars of Western cultural civilization at all but rather Liberace, Rock Hudson, Sylvester, Robert Mapplethorpe, Tony Richardson, Klaus Nomi, the Marquess of Dufferin and Ava and a wide selection of nightclub entrepreneurs, art historians, balletomanes, film critics and fashion designers. To the families and friends of these people, their deaths are, of course, tragedies without equal. But to concentrate so much on the deaths of a few white Western men while Africa is dying of AIDS smacks horribly of a new, acceptable imperialism. AIDS PLAGUE IN AFRICA: NOT MANY DEAD will get two inches on the inside page; Freddie Mercury is a front-page screamer *and* a pull-out souvenir.

Seven years ago, we were worrying about feeding the world; two years ago, we were going global and saving the rainforest. But AIDS, in which we attempt to take care of our own – charity begins at home! – before tackling these tasks perfectly shadows the political cycle of the Sixties and Seventies which started out wanting to change the world – the Peace Corps, civil rights – and ended up in therapy, in the touchy-feely-feelgood racket, insisting that if you changed yourself, the world changed with you. We are all Jane Fonda now.

Rejecting starving Africans in favour of rainforests was an act of staggering callousness; in rejecting rainforests for AIDS, the vicious family circle is complete. For far from being a reaching out to the world's untouchables, the fashion for AIDS expresses a stunning degree of self-interest on the part of the Cause Celebs involved – for the most part ageing ravers who screwed anything that moved (or didn't move fast enough) throughout the Sixties, Seventies and Eighties, and are now living in fear and on a prayer.

The worlds of showbusiness and art have always been amusing in their self-absorption; as they elbow every other charity aside in their frantic search for a cure for their malady – which may or may not be *imaginaire*; it might just be a bad case of Millenniumist's Tic, which is a bit like Housemaid's Knee (except you only get it once in a hundred years) – they have become the stuff of black comedy. Oscar Wilde would have had fun with them. But then, they don't make them like Oscar Wilde any more.

*

In 1990, the first World AIDS Day was marked by a long-playing record, *Red Hot And Blue*. On it, an assembled company of largely heterosexual singers demonstrated their solidarity with the cause by duffing up, without provocation, the best songs ever written by the peerless homosexual songwriter Cole Porter. What this album achieved was not an immediate global conversion to the rank pleasures of the condom, but to highlight the terrible damage that two decades of 'liberation' had wrought upon homosexual creativity. Instead of 'Night And Day', we have 'Glad To Be Gay'; instead of Montgomery Clift, Ian McKellen; instead of Oscar Wilde, Julian Clary. 'Repression is the mother of the metaphor', was one of the great John Cooper Clarke's greatest lines; try telling that to Leigh Bowery. But with young stars such as Lisa Stansfield and Sinead O'Connor, backed by falling stars such as Annie Lennox and David Byrne, it reportedly raised £2 million for AIDS research.

This month, the second World AIDS Day took place, marked by thirteen concerts across the world. Miss Stansfield, Seal and Belinda Carlisle were supported by Marc Almond, Jimi Somerville and Boy George. You know the old MGM slogan MORE STARS THAN THERE ARE IN THE HEAVENS? This was sort of MORE STARS THAN THERE ARE IN HEAVEN THE NIGHTCLUB. *JUST*.

Conventionally-minded AIDS-bores will explain the massive stellar gap between Live Aid and World AIDS Day with the highly misanthropic excuse that pop superstars dare not come to their aid lest the meat-headed public cease buying their records. (Not the same meat-headed public who gave them £2 million last time, presumably.) In any country but England, this might wash. But here, from Bowie to Boy George, it is almost etiquette for a pop star to confess to a liking for his own gender, so much so that many heterosexual crooners have kissed the ring in passing. The only AIDS pop stigma there is is in speaking out against its victims. Soon after Donna Summer, a fundamentalist Christian, declared that AIDS was God's wrath, her career nose-dived when gay club DJs stopped playing her records. She can now be seen recanting on breakfast television for a good part of every year, utterly defeated. Satisfied?

Then there is the theory that the world was gripped with compassion because Live Aid was 'safe' – that Third World famine was beyond controversy. How little the bourgeois dummies know! The Third World's habit of bearing far more children than it could dream of feeding angers even liberal pressure groups; amongst regular folk it can cause blind rage, and a good deal of blame-casting. In short, Ethiopia was hardly the RSPCA; it was far from being a sure thing.

Even if it was a fairly unanimous decision that starvation was a bad thing, Live Aid never *felt* safe in the way other appeals have – and it never felt smug and self-regarding, as do the AIDS pop bashes. There is something flesh-creepingly middle-class about the public face of the AIDS Brigade. If it is a disease that affects 'all' of us, then why are its spokesmen such naice young white men who look better suited to running antique stalls in Brighton? Where are the Glaswegian junkies, the King's Cross prostitutes, when AIDS is debated? We never see them; just the bland young Simons and Nicks of the charities, trusts and commissions.

*

Perhaps the difference between Live Aid and the AIDS Brigade is best summed up by the personalities of their leading lights, Bob Geldof and Margaret Jay.

It was Geldof's hedonistic, tormented persona which made Live Aid so different from a million milksop appeals. He seemed so driven, so close to falling off the edge – it really seemed that like the CSM-101 in *Terminator 2*, or Gene Hackman's muscular priest in *The Poseidon Adventure*, Geldof was more than ready to throw himself into a molten pit, could one be produced, in order to stop starvation's long march – that at times it was as though we were giving to save him as well as the Africans. One down-at-heel, debt-ridden, doubt-ridden ex-pop star (Div II), driven half-mad with passion, made us shell out like sailors on shore leave in a way the decent and drab great and the goody-goody had never done.

There is no passion from the AIDS Brigade, only preaching. They ask both too little of us – wear a condom, not feed the starving – and too much. Geldof wanted your money, pure and simple – he didn't care about anything else you did. These people seek to take away your right to an adult sex agenda and replace it with cold, clammy rubber, vanilla sex and pathetic masturbation; not so much 'safe' sex as pre-sex. A culture which sees mutual masturbation as some sort of adult ideal is a culture that has been well and truly infantilized.

The personification of the AIDS Brigade is its head honcho Margaret Jay. Daughter of Jim Callaghan, ex-wife of Peter Jay, co-respondent of Carl Bernstein (giving new meaning to the term 'relative values'), 'Ms' Jay is Euro-bureauwoman supreme. She does not even appear to have been devised, using graph paper and slide rule, by the same tepid Think Tank which also let loose those towering intellects Tessa Blackstone and Patricia Hewitt on us; it is fair to say that if Margaret Jay did not exist, no one would have dreamed of inventing her.

Only one thing would seem to suit her for her new position: carnal knowledge of Carl Bernstein, of whom his ex-wife Nora Ephron opined that his sexual appetite was so undiscriminating that 'he would have screwed a Venetian blind'. For as we well know, when you go to bed with someone you go to bed not just with them *but with every Venetian blind they have ever screwed!* Disgustingly smug and lightweight, Ms Jay's pronouncements have an unfortunate rebel-rousing effect on one. Just as seeing Simon Bates warning you at the start of a hired video that children under the age of fifteen must not be allowed to view it makes you want to drag your infant out of bed to watch splatter films, so Margaret Jay's lectures on the joy of safe sex make you want to rush out to the nearest public lavatory and consume body fluids by the bucket.

Knowing how deeply bourgeois they are, the AIDS Brigade try to get 'with it' like some trendy vicar. They like to 'hang out' in aid of AIDS; typically, the World AIDS Day concerts were called 'dance parties'. Imagine Geldof allowing Live Aid to be billed as a party in aid of starvation! On one hand, the AIDS benefits tell you to chill out, relax, don't sweat it; on the other, they're screaming at you that we're all going to be dead by the year 2000.

With bad luck and bad judgement, AIDS could happen to you; famine couldn't. The appeal of AIDS charity is the appeal of looking out for numero uno, albeit via the scenic route of brotherly love. Geldof took the gamble of alienating people by telling them to care about something they were never going to be hurt by; AIDS appeals to the selfish why-me-God? whinger in all of us. And its spokesmen are so arrogant and snooty that you wonder if they really *want* your help; look at the high-handed, pedantic rejection of the phrase 'AIDS victims' in favour of the pompous official-speak 'Persons With AIDS'. Would Geldof have insisted that we call the Ethiopians 'Persons Of Limited Calorie Intake' to preserve their dignity?

Far from being too dangerous to evoke public passion, AIDS fund-raising already seems too bureaucratic and conservative to really make us want to tear off our wedding rings to be melted down and sold for grain (as hundreds of dirt-poor rural Irishwomen did for Live Aid) or sell our brand new dream homes (as several young English newly-married couples did for Live Aid). Paradoxically, appealing to public altruism seems to be a better bet, benefit-wise, than appealing to self-preservation. For AIDS aid has taken off as a pet cause (in total income, including legacies, the Terence Higgins Trust takes less than the Donkey Sanctuary. AIDS is, however, massively overfunded by government; in 1989/90, £160,235,000 was spent on AIDS education and research (553 deaths from AIDS p.a.) while in the same period only £9,900,000 was spent on education and research into heart disease (killing 197,721 during this period)) only amongst those who think they have a pretty good chance of catching it; the media-weeny worlds of dance, fashion, alternative comedy and the theatre.

Showbiz folk, by their nature, tend to have far too inflated an idea of their own importance – especially its role in swaying public opinion. If you are going to stage a personality-led campaign, you had better have a big personality at the head of it – that means a Geldof, not a Ruby Wax. (A big mouth does *not* necessarily mean a big personality.)

When Elizabeth Taylor pecked a Person With AIDS chastely on the cheek, a spokesman gushed that 'this does more to allay fears than all the talk from the medical experts!' Says Nick Partridge, another AIDS Brigade spokesman: 'Through the actions of the Princess of Wales, people have realized AIDS is a serious threat, where they might not have taken notice of TV advertisements.' This star-struck, knicker-wetting and highly misanthropic view of the power of celebrity to move the mindless lumpenprole when all else fails does beg the question: then why keep pouring all that government money into the coffers of medical experts and advertising agencies when a bit of face-sucking from an ageing film star does the job just as well?

The AIDS Brigade hopes that in Diana or Madonna it will find its Saint Bob. So far, at the £250-a-head banquets (extremely cut-price, as these bunfights go) AIDS has attracted the 'N' Crowd rather than the In Crowd; Marie 'N' Jerry, Michael 'N' Shakira, Dawn 'N' Jenny – models too old to model, wacky comediennes and bored society hostesses prevail. There is always Princess Marg and Grey Gowrie, of course; but as Stalin might have said, how many divisions do *they* have?

It is, of course, repellently reminiscent of Tom Wolfe's radical chic, as documented a quarter of a century ago. Nothing on earth can convince one that some people are born without any concept of shame so much as seeing the self-serving, cock-sucking slags – male and female, homosexual and heterosexual – of showbusiness running around like headless chickens and preaching 'safe sex' to the 'little people' who always, instinctively, *knew* that extreme promiscuity, ceaseless sodomy and sex with more than five people at once (six is a dinner party, but seven is an *orgy*) led to heartbreak, confusion and Something Nasty in the Woodshed. Poignantly, it is those now telling us how to have sex who should have been listening to us telling them.

'These poor people,' said the art dealer John Kasmin, looking around an AIDS luncheon. 'If AIDS didn't exist, what would they do with their time?' Not much, not much; but it must be a comfort to those plagued by AIDS that their deaths have given a new lease of life to the washed-up, partied-out marked-down AIDS Brigade.

Forty-eight hours after World AIDS Day, Elizabeth Taylor – whose life has been a hypochondriac's wet dream – took to her bed with a reprise of the 103-degree fever pneumonia which almost killed her a year before, cancelling several AIDS benefits in the process.

Mr Larry Kramer, the AIDS activist, writer and Person With HIV Positivity, took this opportunity, while addressing a men's meeting, to call Miss Taylor 'little more than a dilettante. It never occurred to her, who has a daughter-in-law with AIDS' (ex-daughter-in-law, but who's counting?) 'to request a meeting with the White House . . . Singing and dancing is indeed all that is going on here. You must use your bank account, and your talent. That ten years into the plague there has not been one major movie about AIDS is abysmal.'

One could make the obvious point – obvious to everyone but Mr Kramer that is, obviously – that picking on someone when they are very sick is not setting a good example *at all*. You might also point out that the showbiz mentality currently acting as a conduit between AIDS and the mainstream is so hopelessly detached from reality that Mr Kramer sees 'singing and dancing' – i.e. the raising of money for AIDS research – as relatively unimportant, while the making of a film would change everything.

But, most of all, Kramer's outburst is a warning to the British AIDS Brigade that, sooner or later, the legions of dead and dying – 67 per cent gay men, both here and there – come to resent those Others – the Smuggies – who seek to save them. Homosexual men tried, and succeeded for a decade at least, to create not just their own lifestyles but their own life*cycles*. Those lives were not like ours; they were wilfully different. The American feminist Marilyn Frye said it first, in 1983, and said it best: 'Gay men generally are in significant ways, perhaps in all important ways, more loyal to masculinity and male-supremacy than other men. The gay rights movement may be the fundamentalism of the global religion which is patriarchy.' Maybe they should be allowed to create and manage their own deaths, too.

In America, Edmund White has written recently against the liberal tendency to 'falsely suggest that AIDS is all in the family'. David Leavitt – a young, affluent, white male – has written of his anger on reading *The New York Times* – which now runs daily stories about men, women and children with AIDS – which featured 'a young, affluent, white heterosexual woman who said she had contracted AIDS after one night of sex with a bisexual man'. While the American homosexual writer Leo Bersani has described American television AIDS warnings as 'a nauseating procession of Yuppie women announcing to the world that they will no longer put out for their Yuppie boyfriends unless they use a condom. Thus hundreds of thousands of gay men and IV drug users are asked to sympathize with all these Yuppettes agonizing over whether they're going to risk a good fuck by taking the ''unfeminine'' initiative of interrupting the invading male in order to insist that he practice safe sex.'

One wonders exactly what Mr Bersani's beef is here – that women want sex, that women want safe sex, or that a woman might want sex with the same man he's stalking. It does seem only fair to point out that if gay men had agonized about condoms a little more, they wouldn't be up to their capped teeth in trouble now.

Such blasts bode ill for the AIDS Brigade. But what can one do? – they won't listen to warnings, being too busy churning out their own. So let the show go on; let Jenny 'N' Lenny 'N' Di 'N' Madonna knock themselves out in aid of this new dirty little sex war effort – and in the end they'll be spat on by the very people they tried to save.

Never mind – you can't catch anything from saliva. Can you?

Apocalypse Now (Please)
or Listening for
the Four-Minute Warning

. . . .

'We're living in a world . . . where SEX
and HORROR are the NEW GODS'
Frankie Goes to Hollywood, 1984

But it *could* have been Mrs Whitehouse, bless her.

Frankie Goes to Hollywood are interesting for three
reasons, and none of them is Paul Morley. One: they are
the ugliest collection of crooners since Freddie and the
Dreamers. Two: like Prince, in a ruder, less well-behaved
poptext (the reigns of the Rolling Stones or Sex Pistols,
say) they would not seem at all shocking; good timing
as much as good miming has got them where they are.
Three: the Frankies, more than any other working act
(apart from perhaps Prince, with whom they share the
vital statistics of physical unsightliness, mock shock and
sexual flexibility) *see pleasure as apocalyptic*. They believe
that the world will end with a *bang* (bang as in 'an act
of sexual intercourse', not as in 'a loud short explosive
noise') and perhaps a slight post-coital whimper. As
Woody Allen said when he was asked if he thought sex
was dirty, 'only if it's done properly'. The Frankies see
pleasure and the apocalypse the same way.

180

The funny thing is that this thinking tallies exactly with the line of the screaming moral meemies, Mrs Whitehouse and Mrs Gillick, who also see sexual generosity as a sign of the decline of the West. (That promiscuity is endemic to humane societies and chastity to barbaric ones is conveniently overlooked by this lobby.) Make love not war, our amiable ancestors said; to the Afuckalypsists making love and war are practically synonymous.

Prince's Baptist washed-in-de-blood-of-de-lamb background can probably be blamed for his girlishly hysterical and guilt-ridden might-as-well-be-hung-for-a-sheep-as-a-lamb attitude to having a good time (has having fun ever sounded like such hard work as it does in '1999'? I've heard of some lame excuses for partying, but *the end of the world*?) while the twin cities of the Frankies' conception – hand to mouth, hedonistic Liverpool, always torn two ways between the easy sailor fun and money and the censoriousness of the Catholic church (the most Latin American city in Britain, with its poverty, powerlessness, Papism and lust for life) and dour, soured by satanic mills Manchester (Paul Morley as the spiritual Pete Best of the Smiths, anyone?) – have also done their bit in the breeding of the beast. Morrissey, shivering with repugnance, avoids meat – eating it and sleeping with it – and hopes that he will go to heaven; Morley, having read Mr Baudelaire like every back bedroom Northern no-hoper, encourages the Frankies to bang and be hanged – 'To escape from horror, bury yourself in it.' Northern pop attitudes to sex show up very strangely compared to affluent, secular Southern sex mores; George Michael sees sex as neither good-sinful or bad-sinful, but something he does for the sake of his health – and, more importantly, his *skin*. In ZTT's secret heart they sincerely believe that sex is *damaging* to your health – that's why they like it.

Sex with a side order of de Sade – hold the Comfort. Epic, apocalyptic sex with rubber and muscles: that's the way – uh huh, uh huh – they like it. But sex is not the only strange bedfellow to warm the futon for Domesday; every corner of the leisure market has fallen. WAR! HUH! What is it good for? (The Frankies do this one.) How about writing songs about it and having hit records? '99 Red Balloons', 'Two Tribes', 'Eight Days', 'Between The Wars', 'Dancing With Tears In My Eyes', 'Time Zone' – even the immaculate Duran Duran could not resist with that line from 'Please Please Tell Me Now'. Hard core, like punk, was the sound of things falling apart (usually the musical instruments involved) and the rubbing of the listener's face in it: a tantrum that desperately believed it was saying something, *you know, profound* and – please God – *terminal*. Those cut-up records, a funky backbeat, black and sleek as an oilslick, sliced into a speech by Scargill, Churchill, Hitler, Malcolm X, want to make you feel you're doing the dance of death, too. The dancefloor is suddenly Cortonwood, Yalta, Nuremberg, Selma, Alabama; and you are not just another ant-like little nightclubber but the majordomo in the engine room of history.

Every muse is wearing a Katharine Hamnett T-shirt these days; there are apocalyptic sitcoms (*Whoops Apocalypse*), soaps (*The Day After*), films (*Atomic Café*), comic books (*When The Wind Blows*) and operettas (with lyrics by Ian McEwan, an early Afuckalypsist). And, of course, you can build whole clothes collections around the apocalypse; from Miss Hamnett's PLEASE DON'T billboards to Miss Rachel Auburn's YOU DID bag lady à la mode. But incredibly, Apocalypsism – or *Amockalypsism* as I shall choose to call it here, it being a reaction more to personal circumstance and career opportunities than the state of play in Geneva boardrooms – is not always in the raw; it can come in the green clothes of ecology and conservation. You can find a bicepy sort of Amockalypsism in the work of Bruce Springsteen, from the perky 'Born To Run' (not *to* but *from*) to the creepy 'Cover Me', in which a girl is asked to do what the entire US Airforce, dropping more bombs on North Vietnam than were dropped by both sides (*all* sides) in the Second World War, couldn't do: keep Bruce's American Dream intact. Mr Springsteen regards the American Dream as old-fashioned girls regard their virginity; it is literally the most important thing in the world, and demobbing it is a sin which calls for almost Olympian anger and regret.

This sentimental post-My Lai Steinbeckian strain – the American Dream as something from which one inevitably wakes up screaming – can also be found in the new land-locked product of Hollywood. *Country*, *Places In The Heart* and *The River* may well be made by liberals – Lange, Shepard, Field; just taste the rural WASPiness of those names – but their message is *survivalist*, about giving up on central government and staking out to the death on your piece of territory (rather like a tomcat). This is what the fancifully-named Kurt Saxon, ex-American Stormtrooper, now the recognized authority on how to survive the apocalypse (be it Bomb, black or Iranian-induced; he's not sure, like most Amockalypsists) to whom a hundred thousand Americans have sent ten dollars for receipt of his wisdom, says: 'A survivalist has given up on the system itself. It's basically a denial of the American dream – people realize that the game is up.' Left and Right blur and merge in Amockalypsism as they do in Libertarianism; a sure sign of basic structural unsoundness.

Ecology and survivalism both see the City, home of clamorous ethnic deviants and corrupt government, as the root of all evil – the hippies who left Notting Hill for Wales and the West were a perfect hybrid of survivalism and ecology both, and typically dense. (Laura Ashley was dressing girls for the Amockalypse long before Katharine Hamnett, for all retreat from the City is Amockalyptic.) The densest branch of Amockology must be the food snobs; those macropsychotics who see Hell in a cold hamburger. As even the staidest of scientists now admits, 'junk food' – the food being (shock horror) quick, cheap, pungent; poor people's food since time immemorial which has now had the upstart nerve to go public and peddle itself to all sections of society, including the food snobs' offspring – is an *aesthetic* judgement rather than a medical one. No one ever died from eating cheeseburgers – the world's oldest man, Mr Charlie Smith of Florida, breakfasts every day on two shots of neat vodka and dines on a hamburger dipped in sugar – but plenty died from eating macrobiotic. 'Health' food has very little to do with health and a lot to do with silly peasant fears about the purifying value of slogging over a hot stove – and the Amockalyptic Sin City idea that buying food is somehow comparable with buying sex; dirty, trashy, *junky*.

The decline of the West seen in a Big Mac, in divorce or herpes (sex has *always* been about having an itch that won't stop . . .) or other sex aids, in monosodium glutamate, in 'People aren't reading anymore' (despite the fact that literacy and book sales are at an all-time high), in everything from cocaine to Cabbage Patch dolls; the *desire* for the decline of the West seen in the use of the word 'decadent' (which actually means, in the context it is used, *having a good time* – though of course that sounds too trivial and wholesome to inject the reveller with glamour; no one wants to be a Redcoat. Nevertheless, it is hard to be decadent without murdering someone or stealing the Band Aid record) or the anti-heroin campaign – THE SCOURGE – of the *Daily Mirror*, as though recreational narcotics had not been used by every society as far back as the Incas. Every social foible is now seen through the dark glasses of the apocalypse; and a royal pain in the tush it is too.

Why is this, that people try to see the end of the world in the beer and bingo of metropolitan social life? Cocaine and rubber clothes do not herald any significant change in the direction of society, but are just another twist on Real Ale and Monopoly, *just another way to have fun*. Unfortunately, having fun is not half as respectable as being decadent and in decline – and now people know that there *will not* be a nuclear war they try to hear the four-minute warning all over the place; to bring back the sense of BIGNESS that the fear of nuclear war gave them. When you have prepared yourself for the bunker, it's hard to settle for the bistro.

The two oldest, unfriendliest heads of the superpowers it was possible to have faced each other, growled, *and put away their guns*. But you have to pretend you still hear the four-minute warning; people have to make a living, as well as feel good. For example, you can only sell a piece on *Dallas* to the respectable publications if you pretend that it is popular because of some underlying

SEXMONEY Western malaise, the vein of which it taps; not if you admit that it is full of pretty women and villains, and thus popular as such entertainments have been since the earliest Laemmle silents. Next time you read a thesis in which the author claims to have spotted an approaching sign of the times, remember he probably hasn't; he has seen *rent day* approaching, more likely, and he is looking for a four-minute warning to tide him over.

Perspective is the unvanquishable adversary of instant shock status and therefore not popular; but I think a little of it never goes amiss. While fussing about AIDS we might remember that the bubonic plague killed 40 per cent of all Europeans between 1348 and 1377. We might remember that melancholia was officially recognized in Vienna, home of the waltz, with which it has a lot in common; only possible in an environment of hothouse affluence, the lush pleasures of depression are the ultimate time-wasting extravagance – the comfort of suicide always there, like old money to fall back on should all else fail.

Mildly intelligent people – of which the media is mostly composed – feel too much like peasants if they are optimistic; they want to be the cerebral equivalent of pale and interesting. Of course, Bomb culture is a much better accessory than culture plain and simple; of course, it is nice to be stage centre for a change and not stage left. But the Amockalypsists of the West, while thinking they care, are agents of camouflage; to draw attention to tiny Western ailments – *nasty* TV dinners, *malignant* cable TV – is to take space from the real points of the world where something *really* akin to the apocalypse is happening – El Salvador, South Africa. The scraped knees in the playpen, in their monumental conceit, believe that they deserve more attention than the massacres in the real (Third) world.

Last year, a magazine calling itself *Survival* came on to the market; it dealt almost exclusively with young black girls' hair, skin and cosmetic problems yet felt no shame in calling itself *Survival*. We have forgotten what survival is, and see apocalypses everywhere but where they are; like a child avoiding pavement cracks, if we conquer enough mock apocalypses we need never see a real one. I hate the hoarse men of the demi-monde mock apocs, who see the apocalypse as aftershave – splash it on all over, feel big. Like the boy who cried wolf, the four-minute warnings are coming so thick and fast that they lie as benign and balmy as confetti on the Western air. The real thing, if it ever comes, will have its work cut out cutting through the endless, shameless cacophony.

FAGS AIN'T WHAT THEY USED TO BE

. . . .

Simon, for whom the word *decadence* was rivalled only in beauty by *fin-de-siècle*, found that Vivian Violett was alive and living in London. The next day he climbed the stairs of an immense baroque biscuit to present himself in the role of young admirer.

Vivian Violett opened his door, an eminently poetic Kashmir shawl slung around his velvet shoulders, and scrutinised him through a gold-rimmed monocle clamped to the side of his beak and a cloud of smoke and other exotic perfume. The poet was charmed by his guest.

'I do enjoy the company of young people,' he sighed, 'especially when they're as pretty as you . . .'

Simon was struck with sadness; the figure dwindling to a skeleton inside its embroidered shawl had been, by its own accounts, the prettiest boy in London. Already he had noticed in himself a tendency to grow a little older each year.

from *Pink Cigarettes* by Shena Mackay

As Quentin Crisp once wrote, all effeminate homosexuals – at least in his day – grew up dreaming of the GDM; the Great Dark Man. But it is a lesser known fact (as indeed all facts are lesser known than the ones Mr Crisp repeatedly regales us with) that all Neurotic Girl Outsiders of white and working-class blood royal and bone and breeding – at least in my day – grew up dreaming of the GDF; the Great Dark Fag.

The Great Dark Fag was the answer to a girl-child's prayer as she lay in her narrow bed at night, eyes not yet bloodshot from too many bullshots and too much bullshit, no stretch marks on her mind and body. He was the father who didn't want to lecture you, the man who didn't want to maul you and the confidante who didn't want to borrow your suede hotpants. But there was a fat chance of finding him among the steaming slurry of Shitshire; he was sitting in a room in Bloomsbury, smiling crookedly at a glass of absinthe, and you were sprawled sobbing on your s-s-s-single bed (Foxx are big this year) because this was one problem you never saw in *Jackie*: 'Dear Cathy and Claire, where would I find a faggot to be my friend? Yours, Sensitive of Somerset.'

So instead, you met him in your dreams. Like Shena Mackay's Vivian, who showers his young admirer with pink cigarettes and green pistachios, with Pernod and Parfait Amour, your GDF is sweet-smelling, reeking of Turkish gaspers, ennui and some strong, spicy aftershave which you can't quite place – though it definitely isn't the *Burt*, *Hai Karate* or *Censored!* that the male population of Shitshire seem to bathe in daily – but which makes you think of the days when New York City phone numbers had tags like PLAZA and RHINELANDER. He has a high brow, as smooth and pink and irreproachable as a baby's bottom, and curiously – for you are a coarse and somewhat cruel girl – you would never dream of screaming such epithets as 'CHROME DOME!' or 'OI! BALDILOCKS!' at him in the street, prior to clutching at your girlfriends like a drowning man in a three-legged race and collapsing with painful laughter. The GDF is beyond all that; he is simply beyond everything.

He wears maroon and mauve and velvet and smoking jackets and a look of languid, terminal irony. Not just any old irony, you understand – not the sort of irony that terrified teenagers wear like lapel badges. No, the GDF is dusted all over with irony – crossed like a Catholic with irony, religiously, as Gloria Gilbert crossed herself with Chanel No. 5. It is his irony, even more than the names he drops and the wines he picks, that makes you love him. It gives you an interest in common; just like a married couple.

For irony has become inordinately important to you with the onset of adolescence; your friends have hormones, you have irony. It seems to be the one thing which can deflect the anguish of organized sports, communal showers and the *menarche*. Life, which is becoming increasingly embarrassing, is much easier to deal with if you strain it through irony – the muslin of the mind – first.

You haven't as yet – give you a chance, for Frig's sake, you're only fourteen! – heard the Gore Vidal line, 'Irony is the weapon of the powerless', and you're pretty damn sure that once you've got irony properly sussed, no one will ever be able to spot the true, petrified you again. You're wrong, of course; it takes one to know one, and it is a constant source of amazement to you to realize –

sometimes through meeting them, sometimes by reading their biographies – that the people you grew up adoring, believing to be the embodiment of that split second of optimum evolutionary human potential, the most assured and stylish people on earth were, to a type, the biggest messes of insecurities and inferiorities this side of Broadmoor. Inside every great glamourpuss is an NBO screaming 'LET ME OUT! – YOU'RE TEARING ME APART!', and smart people always see it. But for now, you think you've got it licked. You can't see past the Pan-Stik. You cannot see that the *appellation contrôlée* of irony is pain; without pain, it is nothing more than a child pulling faces in a mirror.

So you sit in your room polishing up your one-liners and your irony like a conscript polishing his buttons – but of course, you never meet him. You're forever in the wrong place. Even when you escape from Shitshire, you're forever getting smashed on snakebite dahn va Roxy, where the trade is just *a little too rough* to attract the GDF. (Though looking back in languor, with a somewhat jaundiced eye, you can pinpoint the handful of young pseudo-bruisers who *definitely* knew where the GDFs hung out – especially when the moon was full and the rent was due.)

And as the Seventies sashay by and you grow up, and as the first half of the Eighties sprints by and you grow old, you realize that two things at least are certain in a world that's constantly changing: that Paul McCartney will *never* marry Jane Asher now – and that *fags ain't what they used to be*.

Part of it is simply a talent gap, and you can't really hang a man for being untalented. (It would be nice to have a go, though.) Goodbye George Cukor – hello Derek Jarman; sayonara Noël Coward – aloha Holly Johnson; Cole Porter – Boy George; Leonard Bernstein – Elton John; farewell Tennessee Williams, Langston Hughes, Truman Capote, Oscar Wilde – hi there, Leigh Bowery! I mean, come *on* – what achingly sensitive teen dreamer wants to worship at the feet of the Village People?

But another change was in attitude, and much less excusable. The GDF, for all his faults – and he could be the last exquisite word in both preciousness and snobbery; Noël Coward's relentless bum-sucking beyond the call of duty to the Family Windsor is horrendously awesome to behold – often really did like women. For a long time, especially during the great studio years of Hollywood, behind every great woman was a great fag who taught her how to dress, suck cock and smile for the camera. A lot of the GDF's initial appeal to *you* (one) was that you could easily cast your coltish, doltish teenage self as his latest ingénue; his Gertrude Lawrence, his Carole Lombard, his delicious, delightful Marlene.

The cult of the fag hag grew up for two reasons: firstly because women have always been unhappy with the quality of their heterosexual set-ups with men, leading them to turn to other alternatives (their mothers and their girlfriends, as well as homosexuals), and secondly because GDFs were genuinely very nice to women. The phenomenon of men hanging around with dykes, on the other hand (unless paying good money to eyeball the dirty deed), is unknown; one, because dykes quite rightly aren't very nice to men and two, because men are happy with their position within the heterosexual empire. But straight girls and gay men always found comfort in each other.

With the advent of Gay Liberation, however, things changed and homosexuals seemed overnight to become both less talented and less fond of women. The reason is simple; despite all the garbage talked at the time about the liberation movements breaking down barriers, what they actually did was to build ghettos – 'Let a hundred ghettos grow tall' could have been the motto of the early Seventies. And whereas with blacks turning on whites and women turning on men one could see where they were coming from and was quite tempted to follow them, when male homosexuals turned they turned not on straight male society – whose love of uniforms, boastful sexuality and enthusiasm for exploiting Third World people in the sex industry they took to like ducks to water – but on women.

In the late Seventies Clone, all female characteristics were stamped out and all male ones exaggerated. It was also in this period that the creative output of homosexuals reached an all-time low. It was very possible that the female and creative sides of homosexuality were linked and that when you got rid of one you got rid of the other – throwing the genius out with the genes, so to speak. Anyway, it was a wry girl's joke in the Seventies to say that all men had a feminine side – except homosexuals, who were all man.

The alleged liberation which turned gays macho killed their creativity into the bargain probably for this reason; that they decided it was best to let 'it' all out. Women too were going through this stage, and what it left *us* with was Dory Previn instead of Dorothy Parker, which I wouldn't wish on anyone – not even a fag. Gays were, we heard endlessly, 'angry'; but the advice don't get mad, get even, has rarely been more needed and less heeded. So you're angry, and you scream your anger in people's faces – and then what good did you do? You alienated a normal, frightened the horses and wasted your rage, rage which could have been secreted and alchemized into something wonderful, as repressed people have done since the creative year dot. At the end of the day, there's not a lot to be said for letting your anger out; it converts no one, and it wastes you. Anger is not an alien squatter or demon inside us to be evicted or exorcized; our anger *is* us, and when you let it out you lose part of your drive. Creatively speaking, I think it is safe to say that 'it' is much better left bottled up.

Eventually, of course, gay macho – with its emphasis on scoring and whoring like any red-blooded soldier in a strange town; the median number of sexual partners for a gay male American AIDS patient is eleven hundred – led to the big disease with the little name, and now there are a great many signs that the Ultraman is on the retreat. This can only be a good thing; what the world *doesn't* need now is a double dose of masculinity, and a man who seeks to cancel out the female in himself is riding for a fall, Elsa Peretti spurs or not. One of the great ironies of AIDS is that for all the shunning of femaleness that the Ultraman practised, the great majority of those caring for men with AIDS are – wouldn't you just know it – women.

Will the born-again GDF step into the Ultraman's cowboy boots? We can only hope that the replacement of the Boystown braggarts by the very Cowardly Pet Shop Boys, with their long selection of showcased soubrettes – Patsy, Dusty, Liza – indicates this. Let a thousand fags flourish (I've always thought that the definitive difference which marks the essential good humour of dykes and the essential bad humour of fags is that dykes can handle being called dykes and even relish referring to themselves as such whereas fags are very censorious and arrogant – very *male* – about what they wish to be called) because for all his pride, the Ultraman forced a lot of his brothers back into the closet himself. There was a point in the Seventies when if you didn't want to dress up in a uniform, or screw twenty men a night, or if you wanted to hang out with women, you were made to feel like a *bad* homosexual.

The GDF sensibility is by far the more sensitive: he understands that he is not a woman or a black, that he is not one of the wretched of the earth and that on the contrary his breed have made up a good part of the ruling class of most countries and cultures since history was first written. He realizes that at the end of the day the state of being gay has more in common with the state of being teenage – the heightened sense of drama and the pride in Outsiderdom – than with being a truly oppressed citizen.

And as for the tale of woe which started this long story – well, I hope that the next generation of Neurotic Girl Outsiders find the GDF of their dreams with happier results than I, born too late, did.

There is a rather pathetic postscript to this story, and that is this; suddenly this summer, after a search which started when I was twelve years old, I met the GDF. But after three months of besieging him with notes and gifts and feeling like an Edwardian masher, I get the message. And I see his point – why on earth *should* he want to be friends with a raving homophobe?

Bitter irony! – as Oscar would have said, each NGO kills the thing she loves. But doesn't my GDF understand that it was deprivation that turned me mean, like any spurned working-class child? That I was deprived at a dangerous age of something *far* more important than a mother's love to girls like me? I was deprived of the love of a GDF, your honour, just when I needed it most – society is to blame! Come back, oh glittering and dark!

STARS

MADONNA

. . . .

The Eighties saw the emergence of what can only be called Bourgeois Feminist Triumphalism, exemplified by Margaret Thatcher in No. 10, Martina Navratilova on the clay courts, Joan Collins on TV and strident starlets like Janet Jackson in the charts. But undoubtedly the First Lady of BFT is Madonna. For, suddenly, feminism is no longer merely about the right to free cervical screenings on the NHS. It is about the right to have as much fun, money and clout as the best of men.

As Madonna said when asked about a po-faced feminist's low opinion of her white-slut-on-heat image, 'Oh, I believe in everything they do – but I was too impatient. I couldn't wait.'

Yet Madonna's impatience has been feminism's gain. She drags feminism along casually in her slinking stride like a cave woman who has just killed her dinner. And her predatory pursuit of all that life, love and Securicor has to offer is a good deal more inspirational to young women than those milch-cows mouldering away at Greenham Common, every hirsute inch the passive female stereotype. Madonna inspires in the same way as Shirley Poliakoff with her advertising slogan:

'If I've only one life, let me live it as a blonde.' Never underestimate inspiration as a means of changing people's ideas of what they can do. Every conspicuously independent woman is the light at the end of the adolescent tunnel of lovelessness.

Madonna – one of eight children of a car plant worker and who was six when her mother died – started out with much less than the Wannabes – the pre-teen girl gangs who made up her original hardcore following and broke into cheerleader chants at the mere sight of a camera or microphone: We wannabe rich! We wannabe famous! We wannabe *Madonna!*

Yet only twenty-eight summers have seen her progress from a Detroit cul-de-sac to a Malibu beach house, and from £5-an-hour cheesecake to an £80 million fortune.

But why Madonna? She is beautiful but not that beautiful, a good dancer but not that good, a good actress only when playing herself and an alleged singer. Strength is the answer – just as the very lack of it marked out the embarrassingly vulnerable Marilyn Monroe.

Women attracted to the entertainment industries are usually woefully weak creatures who seek to offer up the old unloved self for a fresh identity and rise like a phoenix. A new name, an official bio and, hey presto, you're born again! Pop starlets tend to be especially insecure, collapsing in a heap of sequins and syringes as soon as the Svengali boyfriend takes his arm away. We've seen it all before, from Veronica Spector to Marianne Faithfull, from Deborah Harry to Annie Lennox. At early Blondie performances, Deborah Harry's shyness was so crippling that she would often retreat behind the amplifiers where she would sing out of sight of the threatening crowd.

The thought of Madonna being troubled by the same neurosis is a howler. In a landscape of wall-to-wall wimps, she is a force of nature, like a hurricane, with so much faith in herself that, sometimes, she appears to verge on the psychotic. Her only insecurity seems to be associated with the built-in obsolescence of the pop star. The fact that Debbie Harry – who had so much more of everything except confidence – could have been consigned so easily to the bargain bin of history must give Madonna a few sleepless seconds.

To combat this, she has tried to keep changing. From the early, sleazy, submissiveness of 'Burning Up' and 'Borderline', through the teasing 'Like A Virgin' to the fully-fledged 'Material Girl', 'Open Your Heart' and 'Get Into The Groove' – from disco bimbo to billboard icon.

But starlets are invariably sexier than stars. Their desperation gives them a raw, itchy edge that often passes as sexual heat. And so the tangly, smudgy siren of the 'Borderline' days was much more attractive than the recently slimmed-down, subtly-shaded model.

That Madonna was also an original, which this year's girl is not. And this should give her some worry. Marilyn Monroe, Jean Seberg, Brigitte Bardot and all the other faces in the hall of fame certainly did not flick through back issues of *Photoplay* when planning their singular looks – they *were* their images.

If all Madonna has up her sleeve for the coming years is an ever more inbred and cross-referring revamp of film-star looks, her future is far from certain. Because any brazen broad with a cleavage and two brain cells to rub together can do that. Some unkind recent photographs show her looking more than a little like a female impersonator: caused by her habit of 'wearing' secondhand looks without really absorbing them. Open your eyes and you're influenced, but influences are useless unless you can improve on them.

And her make-up isn't the only thing that's been given a cleaning-up. Now the past is under the scalpel. Two years ago, she said: 'I thought of losing my virginity as a career move.' Now she sniffs: 'I never slept with anyone to get anywhere.'

Indeed, time may show that Madonna has been as much the ladder as the climber. Association with her did not hurt Steve Bray, John Benitez and Nick Kamen one bit. Her desire to appear the user rather than the used may have led her to exaggerate exactly how useful men have been. Which all makes it more difficult to explain why Madonna, the ultimate victor in the battle of the sexes, is so drawn to Marilyn, the ultimate victim.

To be fair, legions of lazy journalists and picture editors – ever-eager to print yet another photograph of Monroe – have aided and abetted Madonna in her singularly misguided fantasy. The truth is that Madonna is as much like Marilyn Monroe as Prince is like Sidney Poitier. The first two are blonde, the second two are black. Take away the protective colouring and no one would dream of making the same comparison to a brunette Madonna.

The idea of a confused, vulnerable Madonna being smooth-talked on to a casting couch is ridiculous. Marilyn looked like an angel fallen to earth who was making ends meet as a call-girl. Madonna is a broad; big-boned, strong-featured and blowsy. She has the easiness of a Jane Russell, the dominance of a Barbara Stanwyck and the sexual oomph of an Ann Sheridan.

In short, Madonna is about as vulnerable as a juggernaut and certainly no Marilyn. You can believe that men would kill for her, but not laugh at her. If such a state of affairs could exist, Madonna could be *too* much in control. Which is very nice for her – but not for the paying public, of whom there have been noticeably fewer lately. The recent records, 'La Isla Bonita' and 'Who's That Girl' have all the finesse of the Portuguese entry in the Eurovision Song Contest. Her films – more turkeys than Bernard Matthews – show a professional judgement out of touch with reality and a professional guidance conspicuous by its absence.

The young Madonna appeared to believe that beauty was fuel to be recklessly burnt up in the pursuit of goals. The new model seems to think that beauty is there to be preserved at all costs. Inevitably, this renders her less interesting than she was; just another new pop puritan who sings about living on the edge and not giving a damn. Like Bruce Springsteen, Michael Jackson and Prince – whose small-world tax-bracket she shares – Madonna is a health bore; no meat, drugs, alcohol, nicotine or caffeine.

Yet this seems to be merely a cosmetic aid – just more grist to the beautification of the sacred self. 'I never eat flesh – vegetarians are paler.'

What do you say about a girl who steps out of her underwear on stage and throws it to the crowd but who starts each day with a five-mile run? Who sings songs to the joys of hedonism and lives on tofu and soya? You say that here is a girl whose preoccupations are more fiscal than physical.

Her live shows these days have about as much to do with sex as prostitution. In other words, the real orgasm comes at the box office.

'Marilyn Monroe was a victim. I'm not,' she says. But,

ironically, it is the victims who live on and become immortal by making such a bad job of being human; Marilyn, Elvis and James Dean were all weak, flawed and hardly ever in control. The very thing that makes Madonna so successful – her self-control – may paradoxically be the thing that stops her from being immortal. Feminism's gain may be mythology's loss.

The momentum she has worked so hard to build will let her cruise for a bit while she decides between a career of grave-robbing or creation. Though Madonna has not as long as she thinks. For pop's mezzanine floor is littered with the illustrious corpses of those who thought that fame meant living forever.

Madonna's ambition is to rule the world, but now it seems unlikely that she will ever receive even an Oscar nomination. But she's still a good thing. And most importantly, she still looks like a whore and thinks like a pimp. Which everyone knows is the very best sort of modern girl.

IN PRAISE OF THE CASTING COUCH

. . . .

I remember a Seventies party game we wiseacre youngbloods used to play when all the gear was gone. Called No, NO, Nanette!, its object was to imagine the unlikeliest film project Bryan Forbes might feature his wife Nanette Newman in, as was his wont, taking into consideration her gender, age and essential Surreyness. I'll never forget the night I won: 'Bryan Forbes presents *Lawrence Of Arabia*. Featuring Nanette Newman as Chief Of All The Bedouins.' You might remember she would be called upon to sodomize Peter O'Toole; no wonder I won, beating out even *Zulu* with Mrs Forbes – naturally – in the title role. How we laughed! But then, how callously cavalier Fortuna spins her roulette wheel. And as it turns out, it was Mr Forbes who had the terminal titter.

Because his copious celluloid selling of his main squeeze was not, as we dewily believed, the death rattle of Elstree nepotism, but a harbinger of things to come. As we gingerly dip a big toe into the hip bath of the safe-sex Nineties, we can safely say that the conjugal bed – or at least the fraternal futon – has replaced the casting couch as *the* launching pad to stardom. Or rather, to screen visibility (they are far from being the same). But do you know the worst part of this, the completeness of our Seventies smartass humiliation? Now that every actress is a muse and every writer/director a meal-ticket, *Bryan and Nanette's back catalogue is starting to look pretty damn good, dammit!*

Once upon a sign, in a mythical land called Hollywood, where the women were all beautiful and the men were all rich — or had 'room-mates' — a never-ending conga of starlets sashayed in through the front doors of the Big Men and staggered out through the back, lipstick smudged, but smiles intact. And clutched in their sticky little hands was the Holy Grail of the Hollywood hopeful — a short-term contract.

Opportunity had knocked, ball had been played, an itch had been scratched. The next trick was the hardest one of all, and the hardest jury had to be satisfied: the stiffs in the paying seats. If they liked her, she'd swim like Esther Williams; if they didn't, she'd sink, and it didn't matter how many Bel Air lemons she squeezed. And that was the good thing about the casting couch: ultimately, the star was the people's choice. The starlet might start out as a prawn, pink and squirming, in some grandmaster's game, but if she made the man in the mezzanine love her she could turn the tables and have the moguls begging for crumbs. If you could give Joe Blow the hots, you could call the shots.

You might have to lie back and think of Oscar for a while; but one day, if you were good, you'd be able to get up from that casting couch and just walk away forever, not looking back. As Marilyn Monroe said on signing her first big contract, 'That's the last cock I ever suck.' (And you wonder why none of her marriages succeeded!)

You could walk like a man.

But what happens when Jessica Lange stops sleeping with Sam Shepard? Is *she* going to have an adoring cast of millions waiting with a safety net while she holds her career close, takes a deep breath and jumps? Put it this way – since Nancy Allen and Brian de Palma loused it up legally, how many marquees have you seen blaring *her* name in lights?

Despite a great deal of chatter from actresses about autonomy and independence these days, there is a very good reason why they appear such shadowy, feeble creatures compared to the alleged 'creations' of the studio system – which the recent deaths of Barbara Stanwyck and Ava Gardner, two studio starlets who mutated into strong and singular stars, drew stark attention to. This is simply because *they are not the people's choice*. And without this mass assertion of their worth, they are all too aware that they exist solely by the grace of the benefactor snoring beside them each night. Disastrously miscast, they become little more than the little woman mugging haphazardly in Big Daddy's elaborate, budget-busting home movies. *And everyone's looking!* You bet they feel insecure.

Today, being a live-in muse carries all the shame of parasitism with none of its past security. Such relationships are under constant threat from market forces and sneering critics. Starting with Bergman and Rossellini – who could do no wrong apart, and no right together – bedroom/boardroom sleeping partnerships rarely translate into commercial or artistic cred. Because love is blind, especially when squinting down a zoom lens, and one man's meat is another man's box-office poison.

And when Mr Artiste has had one flop too many, there's every chance he'll turn round and blame *you*. Because as a bad workman always blames his tools, a man always blames his broad – and what more convenient arrangement than to find two whipping boys within one self-effacing frame?

It might not even be your fault; did any alleged albatross ever fly as high as Cybill Shepherd after she left the supposedly God-like Peter Bogdanovich? 'They said I was destroying him,' she said earlier this year. 'But he was destroying me.' Shame it took her such a long time to find out. But that's feather-bedding for you.

Such relationships emasculate the actresses who enter into them. But more importantly, they clog up the channels through which new actresses appear. How can the mystery girls, the future Marilyns not cut out to be live-in life-partners and self-sacrificing Significant Others, make it before they're mugged by gravity when so many female roles go to the muse who makes the muesli? – Lynch's Isabella, Hare's Blair, Beineix's Isabelle, Roeg's Theresa, Polanski's Emanuelle or Allen's Mia?

Beyond the emasculation and exclusion of actresses there is, however, a third and more sinister effect that the collapse of the couch and the rise of the relationship has had on modern film. And this is the fact that no man wants to show to all the world the mother of his children as a true blue bitch and ballbreaker on a screen twenty feet high. This might be all well and good – if a little party-pooping – were it not for the fact that, especially in the cinema, an interesting, strong woman is, by her very nature, a bitch and a ballbreaker. Nice girls are just window dressing: go on, you think of a 'nice' female role as famous as Scarlett O'Hara or Mildred Pierce. So these days, all the strong, interesting parts go to Kathleen Turner, Ellen Barkin and Glenn Close; some of the few actresses not involved in master–muse set-ups. Clearly the paying public can handle it – as the success of Everybitch from Joans Crawford to Collins proves. The sensitive little auteurs have more of a problem, especially when it comes to casting Her Indoors in such threatening roles as those played by Turner in *Body Heat*, Barkin in *Sea Of Love* and Close in *Fatal Attraction* and *Dangerous Liaisons*. Never underestimate the *reality* of film to directors: it is they, not the suckers in the cheap seats, who have trouble telling fact from fiction. And this being so, they put their women on the screen in situations they find acceptable in life. In peril, at home, bringing up baby, defending the farm; but *never* on top.

But the accepted wisdom is that the so-called 'Women's Film' – whose forerunners were those gems from the Thirties and Forties directed by George Cukor and Douglas Sirk, starring Joan Crawford and Lana Turner, dressed by Edith Head and Adrian – is back. Last year, a piece in the *Guardian* entitled 'Girls On Film' argued that while the central tenet of my 1986 book of the same name – that women had been written out of modern film by men too terrified by their advances in real life to let them run the show up there on the screen, too – *had* been true, it was no longer. Women, it claimed, were stage centre once more; the Women's Film was back.

I disagree. Yes, there are certainly more parts for actresses than there were six years ago – largely because of the dwindling of the Buddy Film phenomenon (wherein two male leads romped around robbing banks in shampoo-ad soft-focus, while some broad sat sewing at home; had *Gone With The Wind* been re-made in the late Seventies it would have been called *Rhett and Ashley* or *Raging Rhett II*).

But what parts! As mothers, wives, hairdressers, cartoon characters and victims, whether of Mickey Rourke's bit of rough or Reaganomics. And worse still, even those films which go through the motions of putting women in the workplace invariably show career girls as psychos (*Fatal Attraction*), frustrated hausfraus (*Baby Boom*) or simply neurotic. *Broadcast News*, whose heroine Jane Craig was much touted as a milestone for the cinematic New Woman, shows a manic depressive who careers crazily between bombastic bossiness in public, and pathetic self-pity in private, as she cries herself to sleep each night in her lonely single bed, bled dry by the 'demands' of her lucrative job as a television news producer!

The message is clear: *having a career makes women cry*. Which will come as news to the doctors who dole out millions of anti-depressants each year to harassed housewives, not confused career girls. Interestingly, neither of the equally pressurized male leads of the film sits alone blubbing each evening. And even more interestingly, neither did the heroines of the Thirties and Forties. They were too busy making their way in the world to collapse in a puddle of hormones every time the going got tough.

The sad fact is that modern screen heroines are only allowed to act tough if they can ultimately be revealed to be really, deep down, vulnerable. Just like that incredibly smug brassiere ad which showed a power-dressed career girl in a stern suit and a chignon next to a picture of the same girl with her hair and defences down wearing nothing but a smile and a bit of satin: *underneath, they're all lovable*. So you needn't be scared of that bitch who bosses your office; just mentally undress her and you'll soon cut her down to size. Modern films are the same. Women have more power, but more problems; more choices but more chance to make mistakes. Every gain is cancelled out by a complaint. Interestingly, women are unique among oppressed peoples in being portrayed in such a disgustingly patronizing manner; no film-maker would dare show the same of the working class, or blacks.

Only Garbo used to get terminal illnesses; now any actress can. Only Norma Shearer was expected to be the perfect mother; now they all are. Once heroines would kill for their children; now they're expected to die for them. It's the difference between self-defence and suicide; the difference between the Women's Film and the Female Eunuch's Film. And that's what these new films are: films about castrated women, with castrated women, for castrated women.

The Women's Film dealt with women's struggle to get *out* of the home; the Female Eunuch's Film deals with their struggles to get *back* there. The heroines are introspective, domesticated and house-trained; thoroughly in keeping with the Green tendencies of the time which, from a woman's point of view, adds up to little more than getting her back into a Laura Ashley smock and the kitchen, where she can bake her additive-free bread for her hippie husband and breast-feed the baby until he's strong enough to rip open ring-pull beer cans with his teeth. We sneered at power-dressing; wait and see how you like *powerless* dressing.

And it's no good saying that men are being shown going back into the home, too, so that makes it OK; male domesticity does not have the same connotations of surrender that housewifery does. Besides, we should be levelling up, not down, and putting men in the home is no consolation for failing to put women out in the world. It just means we all veg out together.

The so-called new climate of caring which produces these films is actually nothing more than a climate of cowardice, as we hide from the fearful challenges of modernism under the skirts of tradition. It is ironic, when we look at the Hollywood which lined up against Reaganism, to find that it was actually in favour of everything that Reagan portrayed himself as being in favour of: roots, land, the family. As it turned out, its grudge against Reagan was not that he was conservative, but that he was *modern*; he believed in pesticides, the break-up of rural communities and divorced men becoming president. The Hollywoodites, on the other hand, believed in Mom and organic apple pie. Bringing the two together in one handy crusade, Meryl Streep heads Mothers Against Pesticides. Jessica Lange says she wants the word 'Mother' on her tombstone. When it comes to conservatism, Hollywood leaves Washington standing.

It is the same ill-sorted, self-satisfied smugness that characterizes today's actresses, both on and off the screen. One cannot help comparing such Professional Mothers as Lange and Streep to the restless, self-doubting stars of the old Hollywood, from Louise Brooks to Marilyn Monroe, and finding them full of phoney baloney. By their very visibility they are obviously ruthless, driven women – this is a profession with 90 per cent unemployment, let us not forget – and with each hymn to home and hearth, they seem more and more like Marie Antoinette playing at milkmaids. When one sees Mary Steenburgen (who was then fighting a savage divorce and custody case against Malcolm McDowell) smile beatifically around *Parenthood*'s chaotic kitchen – which resembles nothing so much as a crèche in the Black Hole of Calcutta – and smarm, 'I'm good at this!', one longs for Joan Crawford in *Mildred Pierce*, pacing *her* kitchen like a caged animal and baking pies as if her life depended on it, determined to *get the hell out or die*. And then you remember where you first saw the prototype for this new, fulfilled, family-oriented woman: in the latter portion of Bryan and Nanette's *The Stepford Wives* some thirteen years ago. Ahead of their time, as usual.

Once people had sex; now they have babies. In the cinema, having a baby used to be the terrible price you paid for having sex – any night of the week in the early Sixties you could find Natalie Wood contemplating suicide on some drive-in screen because of the interesting condition Steve McQueen or Warren Beatty had left her in. Now, having sex is the terrible price you pay for having a baby.

In the molasses maelstrom of domestic bliss, conjugal nepotism and *thirtysomething* smugness that swamps the modern screen, the loneliness of the short-term contract casting couch seems oddly appealing. And, in its way, *pure*. What both parties wanted was clearly stated, uninflated by relationship-rhetoric. Favouritism never swaddled the hands of the studio heads, whose ultimate aims were fiscal rather than physical; the people's choice held sway, and the public got the stars it wanted rather than the apple of the director's eye. Actresses who made it were seen as their *own* triumph rather than as the back end of some performing pantomime horse who came along with the package.

It was prostitution of a type and, despite numerous attempts to redeem it, prostitution is essentially an ugly business. But it's better for both your soul and your bank balance to sleep twice with a man you despise and get something out of it than to do it twenty times for nothing. And it would be naive to believe that more cruelties are done to women in the massage parlour than in the marriage bed.

Actresses are actually shown much *less* adulation and respect now than when the casting couch was fully operative, largely because of the element of privacy and discretion inherent in the set-up. Joe Public didn't have a clue who Marilyn slept with to advance herself, and no one used to boast of actually *having* an actress while the cameras rolled, as Bruce Dern has of Maud Addams, Jack Nicholson of the pre-Shepard Jessica Lange, or Mickey Rourke of Carre Otis. The humiliation of the couch pales beside such public displays of dominance and submission.

In the old days, when a starlet had proved her public appeal, she was groomed to within an inch of her life and given the best of everything: projects, writers, scripts, directors, roles, co-stars. Nowadays, you have to babysit the ego of some stoned hippie who thinks he's a Renaissance Man and can do it all, then watch as he falls flat on his face; and *you* carry the can for standing by your man.

Progress! All in all, I think a quick ten-minute session once a week for a while with some big-cigar-about-town had a lot to be said for it. And in the end, the results speak for themselves. From the couch, like Venus from the conch, rose a gallery of immortals. From the family futon rose a line of jobbing actresses. Come back, casting couch – all is forgiven.

MARGARET THATCHER

. . . .

'Was she Mrs or Ms?' some misguided soul asked her on her first visit to the USA in 1975. 'I am not sure I fully understand the significance of your question. I am just Margaret Thatcher. You must take me as I am.'

Taking her for what she *ism* has been more like it; Thatcher has become so emblematic of the decade that you can't order a glass of Perrier water in some circles without provoking an indignant geek chorus of 'Thatcher's Britain!' We have become two nations divided by one leader; not so much North/South or rich/poor but rather love her/loathe her. We must take her as she is – but what is she?

In 1979 when she first came to power, no one really took her seriously with *that* voice, *that* hair and *that* husband; she was easy to dismiss as an overbearing, over-reaching middle-class housewife, sleeves rolled up ready to scrub the nation free of the stains of socialism, serving up warmed-over Victorian values and nouvelle cuisine portions of the poor. Ten years later, her intellectual and social betters aren't laughing any more but staggering around like punchdrunk fighters. Duh . . . what hit us?

It is a common mistake to see her resolution and energy

as indicating the lack of a complex personality; strength through simplicity. Every aimless, procrastinating fidget thinks he's Hamlet these days. But the key to Mrs Thatcher is understanding how *untypical* of her class, her party or anything else she is.

Despite the Right-On hysteria, Mrs Thatcher has never been an old-fashioned girl. Voting for her was like buying a Vera Lynn LP, getting it home and finding 'Never Mind The Bollocks' inside the red, white and blue sleeve. She could never understand what all the fuss was over poor Cecil and the Daughtergate scandal, or even over Jeremy Thorpe, whom she barely knew and defended hotly to more strait-laced colleagues. She basically doesn't believe that sex is any big deal; this is why she has proved such a disappointment to Whitehouse, Gillick, Anderton and the sperm-ridden minds of the Right who wanted moral rearmament and got a 2p in the pound tax cut instead.

While the Right-Ons have been disappointed in their self-dramatizing wet dream of Big Sister and her police state, let's hear it for those old evergreens 'Loadsamoney Society', 'Victorian Values' and 'Thatcher's Britain'. These are the cerebral Horlicks of the Left, fulfilling the same catch-all, say-nothing function as 'The Permissive Society' does for the Right. It's a way to pass the buck and blame and avoid thinking too deeply about the boredom and grief of the condition called human; which hurts, whoever's weekending at Chequers.

Otherwise sane friends of mine, some on 45K, still talk about prison camps being set up secretly for trade unionists, West Indians and lesbians. Now this last one sounds like great fun to me, but as I walk down the street looking for the party all I see are government-funded posters warning junkies not to die from dirty needles – poor babies.

Sorry to rock the clichés, but Mrs Thatcher is *not* trying to drag this country kicking and screaming into the nineteenth century; she is a brutalist futurist, a Conservative with no interest in conserving, especially ye olde Englande and its olde industries. She is an internationalist – unlike Labour, who lash themselves into a sentimental tizzy every time Johnny Foreigner puts in a bid for a British sweet factory.

What people forget is that it was not easy, until very recently, being Margaret Thatcher. She is one of those strange socio-economic mutations, like Morrissey, who by the grace of talent and timing have nowhere to go but the top. She is the misfit who made it; at school a loner, at Oxford ignored ('None of us ever thought she would get very far,' said Dame Janet Vaughan, her principal) and, in the Conservative Party, a woman from the wrong side of Watford *and* the tracks. She has always had to take stick for being a woman; from the drunken Tory who asked her at a Number 10 luncheon while she was Edward Heath's Education Minister if there was any truth in the rumour that she was a woman, to the caring, anti-sexist Labour Party and their Ditch The Bitch campaign of 1983. (How would they react to a black Conservative leader – Dump The Coon?)

'What did it ever do for me?' she snapped when asked about feminism; what has she done for us? feminists still bleat. Funny – I thought they didn't like having doors opened for them. *What she has done is prove it can be done*; a smash and grab contradiction of the Labour promise of jam tomorrow so long as you pick the fruit, sister, and stand by your man, even if he is your moral, intellectual and telegenic inferior – just like Glenys.

As a misfit, identifying with one class or gender feels unnatural and claustrophobic; this is why she believes in individuals, not society. Forget the mainland, we are all islands, and the only bell worth ringing is not one in some pastoral English church tower calling the faithful to communal prayer but the one that says, 'I'm on the bus, Jack.' Existential Yuppiedom, anyone?

Mrs Thatcher is not uncaring or cruel, but she is naive. She can't comprehend how absolutely useless, helpless and hopeless a good many people are and is cursed with an incredible optimism and romanticism as to what the individual is capable of. If she kicks away the crutches, it's because she really does believe that everyone has the ability to walk without them.

Like De Gaulle, whom she most resembles, she is a master of illusion who cannot fight crime or reduce the deficit but can make her country feel big. This is supposed to be a bad thing; Neil Kinnock, who would admittedly make a fine leader of Belgium, Luxembourg or another of those little countries whose finest hour comes when they make runner-up in the Eurovision Song Contest, would no doubt adjust us better to our role as third-rate power. But the question arises – third-rate compared to whom? To the Americans, the Japanese, the French and the Germans? Come off it. And with the fall of the great powers, as advertised, our accepted role already seems a shade outmoded. There's a shake-up going on, and who's to say we won't do well?

Mrs Thatcher is no longer a politician but a *leader*, and she's too big now to have her finger on the pulse – leave that to the backbenchers. Poll after poll shows the British to be a collective people scared of selfishness and the social upheaval they are sure it brings; for every issue they agree with her on – Trident, the unions – they disagree on another – American bases, the NHS. It is not, as the Left would have it, that her policies touch a lowest common denominator; Labour, with their nostalgia and protectionism, go in much more for that.

Thatcher is voted for *despite* her policies, and now, despite her politics. She has moved to a place above politics, possibly since the Falklands War, which may be why she gets along so badly with the Queen; Olympus isn't big enough for the both of them. Like Kennedy, Roosevelt and Stalin, she has reached that place between holiness and hologram where no one seriously expects the policies to work but no one can shake the symbolism and what it means to their sense of nation.

Some of it is sleight of hand; we are still being served up to the US, Japan and Europe in bite-sized pieces. But in many ways we are bigger. When it comes to talking to the Russians, Britain has been the effective leader of the American-speaking world ever since the election of the global village idiot Reagan. Because we won our little war, no one will be tortured in Argentina tonight. We are no longer a joke.

She has very little charm, grace or sense of humour, but most women who have this have little else, and besides, she never wanted to be an air hostess. She wanted to be a leader, which she is, taking to the whole eclectic post-modernist mess of cultural relativism a cosh of absolute certainty. It is this, as much as anything, for which the Don't-Knows and Right-Ons of our time can never forgive her; for stopping the sensual and easy descent into the sludge of historical irresponsibility. 'Who won the war anyway?' was a singularly British and uniquely poignant cry; Margaret Thatcher, for better or worse, till death us do part, told them, *you did*.

We tried to be Belgium before, and we weren't happy; Neil Kinnock can only have us heading straight back there. Like the British people in general, I don't believe in Thatcherism but I do believe in Thatcher, given the options. It is to her, not her discredited policies, that there really is no alternative. Send her victorious, happy and glorious. Because it's either that, or going back to getting excited about making runner-up in the Eurovision Song Contest.

GIRLS OFF FILM

· · · · · · · ·

There are many reasons why I will not be sorry to see the final cut of the British film industry.

The first and most important is that, if the truth be told, British films have always been pretty damn awful.

But Hammer, Connery as Bond, *Carry On Up The Weary Clichéd Stereotype!* I hear you cry. Yes, of *course* we were proud of these films – but only because they proved we could still bring in budget-tight commercial corn with the rest of them, if not the best of them. That's being damned with rather faint praise, especially considering the calibre of film coming out of Hollywood at that time – *Spartacus, Imitation of Life, The Manchurian Candidate*.

Ealing! you smirk, secure in having hit me with your surest and slyest slingshot. Ah, yes – Ealing, the Difficult One. Because, truth to tell, how many times have you and I (separately, of course) settled down on a rainy Sunday afternoon with one's bodyslave, a bottle of Bollinger Brut and a box of Black Magic, to watch a Classic Ealing Comedy – only to realize after twenty minutes that it's dull as ditchwater and time once more to send said bodyslave out into said driving rain to hire out *When Harry Met Sally* just *one* more time?

The second reason is that supporters of contemporary British cinema – and for *contemporary* read films about posh boys between the wars or cosh boys just after the abolition of National Service – are a certain, singularly irritating strand of humanity who scream like stuck pigs should they detect one pinch of patriotic pride in *appropriate* things like war and remembrance in a fellow Briton, but come over all parochial in the entirely unapt arena of the arts.

Art is surely the most universal of ideas – yet suddenly there will be much excitable talk about the 'swamping' of our national culture by alien ones (American films and Aussie soaps, that is, but definitely *not* black rap or Asian bhangra – it's only okay to be frightened of swampy alien cultures if they're white) and of having to 'preserve' (by any means necessary – so long as it's not bound up in suffocating compromise, like making films people want to see) the British film industry at all costs. 'Preserve' – as though an art form was not a living, mutating organism, but a vegetable about to go manky. Though in the case of British film, this may be rather closer to the truth than its supporters would like.

Yes, we will fight them on the sound stages of Shepperton, and in the cutting rooms of Pinewood! But if we do not need to preserve our parliamentary heritage, or our currency, or our sovereignty, then why on earth should we get our La Perla Euro-scanties in a twist over a bit of celluloid? If national boundaries count for nothing in the new world order, how much less they must mean in the land of make believe.

But the third reason is the one closest to my heart. And it is this: that no other film industry in the world, not in India, or Japan, or China, or Spain, has treated actresses – you remember, the things that *created* the modern cinema, long before David Lynch was even a sty in Hitchcock's eye – with such cavalier contempt as the British film industry has. This alone is a good reason for it to be allowed to go under. The girls themselves bailed out a long time ago.

Amanda Pays, Patsy Kensit, Rachel Ward, Greta Scacchi, Joanne Whalley, Charlotte Lewis, Sadie Frost – Britain now exports beautiful young actresses to Hollywood at the rate Italy did in the Fifties. The irony is that even in war-torn Italy, Sophia Loren and Silvana Mangano, Claudia Cardinale and Gina Lollobrigida were able to build better careers than a British-based actress can in the affluent Nineties.

And in the Sixties, France was synonymous with sexy actresses – but very few of them bothered to go to Hollywood. They didn't need to; Simone Signoret, Jeanne Moreau, Françoise Dorléac, Catherine Deneuve and, of course, Brigitte Bardot became world-class stars without leaving home. Bardot was particularly contemptuous of Hollywood; in 1965, she was offered ten thousand pounds – a lot in those days – for five minutes work at the end of the film *Dear Brigitte*, the story of an eight-year-old American child protégé who is in love with her. She refused to leave France; in the end, the entire cast and crew – including James Stewart – were forced to fly to *her* for five minutes of film. Later, she was furious to find that her contract for *Viva Maria!* included a clause promising that she would visit the USA for promotion purposes. She went, but behaved badly.

Bardot's agoraphobia never limited her appeal – longer and stronger than any female Hollywood star of the Sixties

– and now, approaching sixty sozzled in red wine and sizzling in the sun, working tirelessly for animal charities and blasting off annually about the perverts and lowlife 'ruining' her beloved St Tropez, her distinctly European destiny seems far more attractive than that of her American counterpart; women past the menopause exercised, dieted and operated on unto a state of youthful middle age, abstaining from all pleasures of the flesh, teetering from AIDS lunch to AIDS lunch. The sex kitten alone has turned out to be an eccentric old woman of character.

The post-war Europeans became stars not because of government subsidies – name me one star who was ever subsidized! – but because the writers, directors and producers who shaped their countries' film industries groomed, cast and billed women for stardom. Whether it was Sophia Loren in *Two Women* (for which she won the Oscar), Catherine Deneuve in *Repulsion*, Anita Ekberg in *La Dolce Vita*, Monica Vitti in *The Red Desert*, Jeanne Moreau in *The Bride Wore Black* or Bardot in *La Vérité*, Euro-girl was on the loose, on the edge and on the make – but always stage centre, and without exception a character of unfathomable complexity.

And importantly, these women's beauty did not – in the contemporary Anglo-American way of seeing things – make them brainless bimbos unworthy of roles that required real acting ability, but perfect for them. The VistaVision vamp – bewitching, bothersome and bolshy – lived on in Europe long after Hollywood ceased to be man enough to deal with her.

In the late Fifties and early Sixties, French stars like Bardot, Deneuve and Signoret thought nothing of popping over to London to make films. But by the mid-Sixties, this most efficacious of cultural exchanges was at an end.

Because in the Sixties, British film became irretrievably masculine; the allegedly Angry Young Men – who I always felt would have benefited greatly from six months National Service and a course of Evening Primrose Oil pills – saw women as nothing more than honey traps which held you down while the system made mincemeat of you. In all of the 'great' British films of the time, Laurence Harvey, Alan Bates and Albert Finney are time and time again prevented from going on to find a cure for cancer by getting Jean Simmons, June Ritchie or Rachel Roberts pregnant.

That these young women too might have had aspirations to something better, and that the pressure on working-class girls to mindlessly conform is even greater than it is on boys, is not once countenanced or explored by these supposedly 'realist' films. You only ever get one side of the story – the *man's*.

The great irony of British film is that the much-mocked era of the stiff-upper-forelock *did* recognize that women could have personalities and passions; Margaret Lockwood in *The Wicked Lady*, Celia Johnson in *Brief Encounter*, Virginia McKenna in *Carve Her Name With Pride*, Anna Neagle in *Odette*, and Vivien Leigh in anything. But with the advent of the Angry Young Men, the Feisty Young Femme was history.

The British film industry of the Sixties found the time and resources to create many male stars – Michael Caine, Terence Stamp, Dirk Bogarde, Peter Finch, James Fox and David Hemmings as well as Finney, Harvey and Bates.

But amazingly this industry seemed incapable of supporting more than one female star: Julie Christie, a more bovine Bardot, and even *she* had to hotfoot it off to Hollywood in order to find more challenging work.

The other promising young starlets were not even allowed the luxury of a role like *Darling* as a launch pad to fame and fortune; girls like Judy Geeson, Angela Scoular, Susannah York, Carol White and Shirley Anne Field were confined firmly to the sidelines, and soon retired into television, multiple marriages and half-hearted stabs at Hollywood. Charlotte Rampling, Jacqueline Bisset and Jane Birkin, who have since become international stars of some status, had to go to France and Italy to make it, such was their unsuitability for playing retarded, knocked-up Northern mill-girls.

It was in the Sixties that becoming an actress became a last resort for the biggest and best British beauties of the day, and girls such as Jean Shrimpton, Celia Hammond, Paulene Stone and Patti Boyd became models instead. Tellingly, after years of refusing film offers, Jean Shrimpton finally made the par-for-the-course turkey *Privilege* in 1969; her role was a typically complex and meaty one, requiring her to trail around after a pop-star-turned-Messiah and look depressed. A definitive Sixties role model, this role made modelling look like Method acting; overcome by the sheer challenge of the project, Miss Shrimpton's hair fell out. Always a clever woman, and refreshingly free of hippie hyperbole, upon the completion of this monstrosity – perhaps the first 'disaster' movie, in that it was a complete disaster – Miss Shrimpton gave up showbusiness altogether and ran away to Cornwall to run a hotel.

Soon after, the British film industry was pronounced dead for the first time.

Of course there is no business like showbusiness for piling on the agony, and reports of the cinema's death have been greatly exaggerated. But its decline is beyond debate. In 1946, there were 1,500 million admissions to cinemas in Britain and the US; in 1986, there were 86 million. What happened between these two dates was, of course, television, in the Fifties. But what happened in the Sixties – the almost total alienation of half the cinema-going population (women) by a smorgasbord of sex and violence so sick and convoluted that it was difficult to know where one ended and the other began – sealed the fate of the cinema. As women made gains in real life, so directors seemed to feel the need to punish them up there on the screen; the female audience, working on the basis that if they wanted sex and violence they could get it at home, for free, voted with their BTMs. The Seventies served up a steady diet of 'buddy', detective and 'action' films, women doing duty as peripheral whores, bores and doormats, and the cinema's decline continued.

Since the Fifties, women have been *bred out* of films, as though they were some sort of mongrel strain – and the result has been steady but sure artistic and financial bankruptcy. The more macho a film gets, the less money it makes; in the Thirties, Mae West saved Paramount single-handed while in the Eighties the mega-macho director Michael Cimino *broke* United Artists single-handed with the Western *Heaven's Gate*, which lost $42 million. Even Carolco, the independent company responsible for the *Terminator* films, is up to its state-of-the-art eyeballs in debt.

Then, in 1990, something happened. A low-budget Disney film, *Pretty Woman*, was made for under $20 million and took $170 million in its first four months. *Ghost*, soon after, took $163 million in three months. With no special effects, no megastars (Patrick Swayze had made three straight-to-video flops between *Dirty Dancing* and *Ghost*, Richare Gere had slashed his asking price by half after a string of failures, Julia Roberts and Demi Moore were struggling second bananas) and no hype, these films knocked the big-budget blockbusters into a cocked canister and went on to become two of the most successful films of modern times.

And they did so simply by attracting back the lost female audience. For the first time since *Love Story* and *The Sound Of Music* – the very atypically female-orientated top box-office hits of the Sixties – the phenomenon of the 'female repeater' was noted: the woman in the 18–40 age group who returns to see a certain film up to a dozen times, often with a large group of female friends. It would seem that women are by nature more faithful – at the box office, that is.

Since then, Hollywood has turned with a vengeance on macho films; the only big buddy movie of recent months has been *Thelma And Louise*. Everything touched by Sylvester Stallone, Robert de Niro, Bruce Willis, Don Johnson, Dustin Hoffman and even Robert Redford turns to fool's gold; only the *Terminator* films earn their keep, as the cutting edge of Arnimania.

And who is Terminator's sidekick? The waitress turned visionary guerilla Sarah Connor (Linda Hamilton) who starts out 'not being able to balance my chequebook, let alone save the world' and ends up doing just that. It should be a matter of some concern to 'serious' filmmakers both here and abroad that no 'serious' film of recent years has given us any female characters as complex and capable as Sarah Connor or Clarice Starling, the young heroine of *Silence Of The Lambs*.

Starling is a working-class redneck girl turned FBI hotshot; her origins are something of an embarrassment to her until she is made aware of her capabilities by the evil Dr Lecter, her very own head-hunting Henry Higgins. Foster, a Harvard blue-stocking, has been asked why she usually plays working-class women such as Clarice, the raped waitress of *The Accused* and the single mother of *Little Man Tate*, and has said, 'I'm drawn to working-class characters because drama comes from people who are in trouble, and who have to work hard to survive.'

Are working-class women, being at the bottom of not just one but two heaps, more interesting than other putative characters? They're certainly the stuff classic Hollywood was built on, from Garbo's hookers through Crawford's blue-collar Medusas to Marilyn's gold-diggers. And in the past few years, after losing out to middle-class hippie chicks like Katharine Ross and patrician poseuses like Faye Dunaway in the Sixties and Seventies, they're back with a vengeance. See Julia Roberts in *Pretty Woman* and *Dying Young*, Demi Moore in *Mortal Thoughts* and *The Butcher's Wife*, Annette Bening in *The Grifters*, Kim Basinger in *No Mercy*, *Fool For Love* and *Nadine*, Michelle Pfeiffer in *The Fabulous Baker Boys* and *Frankie And Johnny*, Susan Sarandon and Geena Davis in *Thelma And Louise*, and in fact *anything* with Susan Sarandon, Sally Field, Jessica Lange, Debra Winger, Lorraine Bracco, Ellen Barkin, Laura Dern or Cher. In fact, it might be easier to list those actresses who have *not* flourished on the wrong side of the tracks in recent years;

the 'classy' Meryl Streep and Diane Keaton, and the vapid rich men's playthings like Bo Derek and Pia Zadora, now both fit only for low-budget high-camp.

In some of these films – *Dying Young*, *The White Palace*, *Rambling Rose* – working-class women are not shown simply as being equal to others, but actually *superior*; sexier, more spontaneous and unpretentious, and bringing an emotional honesty and lust for life to the stultifying existences of bourgeois boys lucky enough to tangle with them. In some cases, such as *Dying Young*, when Julia Roberts' blue-collar angel makes a rich boy forget he is dying of cancer simply by introducing him to redneck pleasures like country music, this can go a little too far. But it also shows that 'willingness of the heart' which Scott Fitzgerald said characterized America – a willingness to try life a different way.

Roberts is currently America's sweetheart; considered the sexiest thing on two legs-up-to-cheekbones. As the likelihood of her being cast as blue-collar beauties shows, America does not see working-class women as figures of fun, as British films do. Over here, they have barely progressed from the battleaxe with the tea urn who provides the comic relief to Celia Johnson's romantic heroine in *Brief Encounter*; even when played by young women like Julie Walters or Margi Clarke, they are always *characters* – filmspeak for caricatures. They are never sexy, or complex, or real; they are a drag queen's wet dream of what a woman is like. Is it any wonder Joanne Whalley had to do a runner to Santa Fe? With that Manchester accent, they'd have had her playing Widow Twankey by the time she was forty.

The moaning Greek chorus will counter that there has

been no revival in the blue-collar goddess on this side of the Atlantic because of the horrid stingy Tory government. But there seem to have been projects and money a-plenty over the past five years to create starring, sometimes Oscar-nominated roles in British films for *actors* as: working-class gay skinheads, Asian gay entrepreneurs, working-class white male drug-dealers, Caribbean working-class gay men, paraplegic men, gay kings of England, gay public schoolboys, working-class retarded police-killers, psychotic gangland twins (one gay), and runners.

The big female roles? Those in *Dance With A Stranger*, *Scandal* and *Mona Lisa* – whores, whores and more whores. And to add insult to injury, the whores in the last two were simply ciphers, suspiciously peripheral to their own stories; we learned far more about Bob Hoskins' character than that of Cathy Tyson's Simone, far more about Stephen Ward than Christine Keeler. Such female characters are inevitably described as 'enigmatic' – a nice way of saying the writer couldn't be bothered to characterize the part properly.

At present, there are more challenging roles in British films for dogs than there are for actresses. If you think you could play a gay, working-class, sporting, public school-educated, Asian-Caribbean paraplegic with a twin, a psychotic streak and an arcane claim to the throne of England, on the other hand, stick around.

From the White Linen films to the Cloth Cap flicks, from *Chariots Of Fire* to *Let Him Have It*, the buddy film is alive, though not well, and dying on its feet in England along with the British film industry. And while our cinema continues to ignore more than half its people, it deserves no aid from us.

DI HARD: THE POP PRINCESS

. . . .

'Faces bloated with cheap confectionary and smeared
with chainstore makeup . . . open sagging mouths
and glazed eyes . . . when *I* was sixteen my friends
and I heard our first performance of Beethoven's
Ninth Symphony. I can remember the excitement
even today. We would not have wasted thirty
seconds of our precious time on the Beatles and
their ilk.'

(Paul Johnson, 1964)

[On seeing a Danielle Steele novel on the bedside
table of a hospital she was visiting, to invalid] 'Oh,
I've got that one! I loved it!' [In more serious tones]
'Unfortunately, my husband disapproves of my
reading taste. He doesn't like me reading light
novels.'

(The Princess of Wales, 1986)

For as long as most of us can remember, Windsor-
watching – a sort of version of train-spotting while both
tugging the forelock and getting fucked up the ass
simultaneously – has been strictly for the nerds of all

heights and incomes; from the simpering knee-high prat with the princess's posy to the grandest pantomime Dame of them all, Barbara Cartland. That is, Royal-rimming has always been incredibly *common*; clever people just couldn't be bothered.

But slowly, over the past decade, something has changed. William Blake told us that a tear is an intellectual thing, and there is nothing like a sob story of love gone wrong – Romeo and Juliet, Trist and Izzy, Scott and Zelda – to create an illusion of classical tragedy where before the fall was seen only another human interest story. When the Lady Diana Spencer married that bachelor grey the Prince of Wales in 1981, the media went wild – she was, after all, the first decent-looking woman to marry into the Hanovers since Katharine Worsley became Duchess of Kent a quarter of a century before, provoking similar 'ere-we-go- hysterics on the English Rose Vs Dodgy Foreigner Princesses theme.

But the intelligentsia stayed cool. It is only since around 1985, when the marriage is widely believed to have sustained damage, that movers, shakers and leader writers have stampeded out of the closet offering advice at a penny-a-line. Norman Stone, Paul Johnson and A.N. Wilson all came down from their library ladders and out of their poker games to grab the biro baton from the sob sisters and turn a masculine eye on the problem. Interestingly, their advice has been almost identical to that of the women they so despise: cheer up, you boring old bastard, and give her one for England.

Very few pieces of writing on the subject have deviated from the numbing norm; one, because of the extraordinary speculation around the extent of the Princess's co-operation, is Andrew Morton's new book

Diana: Her True Story. And the other was a brilliant piece by the *Evening Standard*'s theatre critic Nicholas de Jongh last month, wherein he reviewed, as one might a first night, 'Prince Charles and Princess Diana performing together in public' at the Seville Expo '92:

> For years the press have hatched synthetic dramas about the Royal Family. But now the Prince and Princess of Wales appear to be staging their own personal drama in front of an audience of millions, and no one can quite believe it is happening. From my seat in Seville Cathedral I had a clear view of them, for eighty minutes. Their performance – as chief listeners and guests – was, of course, wordless and entirely proper. But right from the first moment, I found the sight of the Waleses rather disquieting. You could see the air around them frosting over. You could sense the chill yards away.

De Jongh is not the usual Royal reporter; on the contrary, he is an earnest cove much taken with homosexuality and AIDS, and theatrical manifestations of such. Yet he devoted a whole page to his sighting of the couple, with a reference to *All's Well That Ends Well*:

> She, like Helena, is the bright particular star who married above her station and rose still further. And her bright particularity – although it is not of the intellectual kind – has become so acute that it perhaps threatens to leave the Prince a little out in the cold. May her popularity not cause him to wonder why he, the thinker, the man of provocative ideas, should be less cherished than she? It is the kind of

dilemma with which matinée idols, playwrights and fashion icons all have to contend when they reach their forties . . .

Later de Jongh referred to Racine —

Duty and not passion, as the strict and restricting dramas of Racine insisted, has to prevail, despite what goes on or off behind the scenes. Why then do the Prince and Princess of Wales show every sign of bringing into the public domain that which is supposed to remain concealed? That is the most tantalizing aspect of the public drama they have now fashioned. Marriages, especially royal ones, come plummeting down to earth. But people usually put on a show. They act the part. They make do

— and concluded that like two Pirandello characters they were 'trying to change the roles they had been given, knowing they could not and consumed by sadness and resentment at the state of things.'

The now very real rift — so real that people are trying to find fictional metaphors for it — in the Wales' marriage has been traced to may things: his liking for the company of 'worldlier' women (though it is harder to imagine a more worldly upper-class young woman than the P.O.W. who told a stunned John Malkovitch 'I'm not easily shocked' when he apologized for the sex scenes in *Dangerous Liasons*, which they were about to see), their difference in age (actually only six years more than the national average), and, most snidely, their intellects. But if the truth be told, there is a great deal of evidence that she is far 'brighter' than he; she may have received only one school commendation – for Best Kept Hampster – but his truly bog-standard degree, after the best education the Civil List could buy, could be seen as a cap and gown equivalent.

Besieged by the press during her engagement, Diana Spencer said, 'Don't make me sound like a bookworm, because I'm not, but I'll read almost anything I can get my hands on, from women's magazines to Charles Dickens. I read because I enjoy it.' Historically, this attitude to books is found far more often among the naturally bright – think of the intellectual's eternal love of detective stories – than the rather pathetic, phoney, posey, adolescent cramming of Solzhenitsyn and Kafka which characterizes her husband. Those aren't books you *read* – they're books you *wear*. Their IQs are perfectly compatible; their difference is that he is *pretentious* and she is not. (And are we seriously to believe that the Prince craves 'intellectual companionship' when the women he rejects his wife for are Camilla Parker Bowles, Dale Tryon and Selina Scott? Come on! That's like joining a Parchman Farm chain gang in search of a slap-up lunch!)

The differences between them are, above all, cultural. It is not the case that Princess Diana is the first 'modernizer' of the Royal Family – Queen Victoria in the last century and the present Queen in the Sixties went a good way towards making the dynasty the Family Firm it is today, with their attention to media and public relations. But Diana is the first Royal icon raised on and sustained by Pop culture. She is our Pop Princess.

This goes far further than the string of spats with her husband over her reading habits, her lack of interest in the visual arts and her love of cheap music – most memorably, when she came onstage during Wayne

Sleep's 1985 Royal Opera House show and did a three-minute routine with him to Billy Joel's 'Uptown Girl'. This included several 'high kicks' over the head of Sleep, who is eight inches smaller than the Princess, which made the unprepared Prince Charles 'nearly fall out of the Royal box', the dancer laughed later. They took eight curtain calls. But the curtain had only just gone up on the new Diana, to whom the world was now literally a stage.

The Princess's Popness can also be seen in her immediacy, her entirely fresh and open emotions and her impatience with protocol – in fact, everything that makes her so lovable and loved (last year she overtook the Queen for the first time as most popular member of the Royal Family). She is, of course, a great showman, but there is nevertheless the feeling that she is the one member of the ruling house who is actually happier among *the* people than among *her* people. The only member of the Royal Family not to wear gloves when shaking hands – though interestingly, she will wear them at family occasions; this is not a phobia, but a *choice* – she endlessly takes on new public engagements and *only ever skives off on family leisure time*, especially when stuck away at Sandringham or Balmoral. Her smiles of elation and tears of compassion when with the young, old or sick are a stark contrast to the look of sheer boredom which can cloud her face during family parties. Like all great stars, she is only truly alive when performing.

Her Popness can also be seen in her pet charity, Relate (the marriage counselling service which sounds like a condom). Not for Diana the stiff upper lip and stiff G&T attitude to disappointments of the heart; she is as touchy-feely psychologically as she is physically. In many quarters, her new and alarming habit of drawing media attention to her loneliness – Poor Me by the Taj Mahal, while His Nibs is off with Sir Laurens; Poor Me by the Pyramids, while Laughing Boy's off with Selina – is seen as an attempt to precipitate discussion and change with an increasingly remote husband. 'If you want to send a message,' said Sam Goldwyn, 'use Western Union.' Diana uses the Western World's global media.

That the Prince of Wales is the great anti-Pop icon of our time, constantly harping back to a golden age when peasants were poor but happy and one's wife didn't jive with Robert Kilroy-Silk, Tom Selleck and Neil Diamond, and that *she* now outshines Madonna as Pop's brightest spark, is what makes their marriage such a unique sham – and so very interesting to those of us who would not normally give a tuppence or a toss about Royalty. In their hasty mismatching – 'When are you going to get married?' Prince Philip is reported to have barked at his son the year before he became engaged, 'If you don't get a move on, there won't be any women left!' – and long repentance lies a great modern tragedy of mistaken identity, and of actually believing that Home is where we come from rather than where we choose to go.

It explodes the myth that roots *do* count, the great self-pitying conceit of third-rate moderns, by showing us that this marriage of two English aristocrats, who had played on each others' estates as children and whose very union was masterminded by their bosom-pal grandmothers, is as unworkable as a marriage between Madonna and the Pope based on the fact that they are both Catholics. Much is talked of the 'firm foundation' that successful marriages must be built on. But marriage is not a stolid stone monolith; it is a fluid, mutating T-1000 of an awfully big adventure. Built on too firm foundations which find it impossible to yield, it will crack wide open.

See Diana run; faster and faster, Princess Toadstool unbound, as she enters the third and most dangerous level of this incredible world she has made for herself. Like some fantastic video game, an ordinary kindergarten teacher from Northampton has become a magical being with the ability, it sometimes seems, to decide whether the richest family in the land rules or perishes, if the greatest country in the world will be a republic by the end of the century.

At her first level, she was Princess as Pop Fan, calling up Capital Radio to wish DJs happy birthday, queuing at McDonald's, screaming on the water chute at Thorpe Park. This alone in a family which had always drawn the common pursuits line at horse-racing (which the aristocracy gave to the poor, anyway) was (as the Lady Diana Spencer said about her then fiancé) 'Pretty amazing'.

Then came the Princess as Pop Star, copied, screamed at, smiling from magazines. She met celebrities as one of them, and they were often unbelievably coarse. 'We shall get you a part in *Dynasty* when you come to Los Angeles,' Joan Collins said. 'She's beautiful – tall, blonde – just my type!' leered the unspeakable Rod Stewart after meeting the Princess in one of the eternal pop line-ups for the Prince's Trust she seemed to spend the mid Eighties shaking hands with. Bryan Adams wrote a song for her: 'Diana/What you doing with that guy?/ He may be a king/ But that ain't everything/ Diana, I love you!' God, bring back the Goons!

Just as this was getting wearing, a new Diana emerged

from the lurex and lip gloss: Princess as Pop Svengali. Perfectly catching the *Zeitgeist*, she became more serious – almost statesman-like. Her speeches (Richard Attenborough was her voice coach) began to drive the prannet-like pontifications of her husband from the news pages. Some people said she had planned it that way.

What was Svengali-like was the unique way she had – has – of managing the press; unequalled by anyone, let alone clod-hopping *ingénues* like Madonna and Prince. The Family had used the press to leak bulletins before. But no one member of the family had ever used the press against another member, as the P.O.W. seems increasingly to do. After the initial post-honeymoon period tantrums and tears, she has settled into a mutually supportive arrangement with the media which seems to give her far more pleasure than her actual marriage. On her recent Egyptian jaunt, she threw a cocktail party for them: when the elderly *Sun* photographer Arthur Edwards fell ill, she took him medicine. When she notices a missing face, she asks if the reporter or photographer has moved on to greater things. 'You won't need me, now you've got Fergie,' she teased a hack pack after the York's marriage.

Her preference seems to be for the tabloids: 'You're from the *Financial Times*? We took that at home,' she told a preening hack. 'Yes, I believe we used to line the budgie's cage with it.' On one occasion she amazed assembled newsmen by asking them if they remembered what a large bosom she had had as a young woman. When Arthur Edwards derided a gown she had worn before, she shot back, 'Arthur, I suppose *you'd* prefer it if I turned up naked.' 'Well, at least I could get a picture of you in the paper that way,' he countered.

She is their creature, and with them she conspires to

win even more power. At times, it could be a more refined, relaxed Madonna talking: 'Oh, you should have seen those Arabs going ga-ga when they saw me on the Gulf Tour,' the journalist Judy Wade once heard her swank to a pack of hacks. 'I gave them the full treatment, and they were just falling over themselves. I just turned it on and mopped them up.'

It is ironic that the woman held up as the ultimate wife and mother was actually *more* domestic before her marriage; hers is now a hot, modern, media career. And getting better every day, as her husband's declines. Attempting to play her at her own game, his recent TV jaunt to live amongst 'ordinary' people on a remote Scottish island was universally reviled as Marie Antoinette playing milkmaids *and* having the nerve to film it.

Statistics show (she said) that the careers of women in bad marriages get better; the careers of such men get worse. But Diana's very success is her next challenge – where does she go from here? After having the love of the world, is there any way that isn't down? – dead on an unmade bed at thirty-three with dirty fingernails after last rites of Southern Comfort? No; Diana has lived a pop star's life, but would never die a pop star's death. *Breeding*, you see.

What does seem likely is that she will flex her power more and more, within the Family in general and her marriage in particular. She will continue to enjoy the pop life she loves, and to use the global media to make her displeasure clear to a husband who can only retreat further and further into the thankless task of simply waiting for his mother to die. At one time, in her sweet and successful attempts to educate herself on social problems, she seemed to be inviting the Prince to see what a great team they could have been. But his sulking and petulance, both of singular proportions, have probably put paid to that.

She is now, in effect, a single parent – and seems quite happy that way. To ask the Waleses to play Happy Families is by now utterly futile; on the water rides with her two sons and handsome detective, she looks like the matriarch of the perfect, high-protection-profile modern nuclear family. (Of *course* that's a gun in his pocket, silly – but you bet he's pleased to see her.) Once we thought that the Wales' marriage was a tragedy because we believed that his wife and family were saddened by his long, voluntary absences; increasingly the tragedy – for him, at least – may well be that they don't give a damn.

Mustn't grumble, though; chin up, on with the Body Shop slap and make sure the cameras get your good side. The Royal roadshow must go on, and whatever warmth and love is missing from the princess's marriage is more than made up for on the world stage. See her, beautifully grave and still in black at the Cenotaph; sweeping up a small black child with AIDS at a Harlem day-care centre, to the amazement of both its staff and her bodyguards, to drive the little girl through New York in her limousine; weeping unashamedly at the bedsides of the dying. She has gone far beyond being a consort now, or even one half of a celebrity couple: *she is the point.*

Far beyond being a Windsor, Diana has become an icon of sexy saintliness – the Church of England at play, in high heels. She is Madonna crossed with Mother Theresa – a glorious totem of Western ideals. Like it or not, P.C. or not, the crowds who turn out to touch her see a dazzling white goddess bringing the benediction of birth control and beauty hints to an ambitious, agonized Third World. Her husband would only choke on her dust.

Twelve years ago, the marriage of Prince Charles and the Lady Diana Spencer was described as 'fairytale'. But it was doomed from the start. This is the man who, when asked if he was in love with his radiant teenage fiancée, said, 'Yes – whatever "love" means.' And this is the girl who, to soothe the nerves of her dressers as she stepped into the Glass Coach which would take her to St Paul's Cathedral, serenaded them with 'Just One Cornetto'. In him, all the anal-retentive agonizing of po; in her, all the unpretentious energy of pop. It could never have worked. Never mind; we didn't lose a prince – we gained a queen. Diana, Princess of Wales, now has the collective cock of the House of Windsor in her pocket, and whether she will show mercy or show out is anyone's guess.

'Get a life' goes the saying – and no one ever got a life as dramatically and drastically as she. Whether it is the life she will tolerate for ever we cannot know. But one thing is sure: whatever she does, for the first time ever the love and loyalty of the people has shifted irretrievably from the ruling house – until death, beyond divorce and dishonour – to one individual. To the one and only People's – and Pop's – Princess.

NATURE, NURTURE OR NIETZSCHE?
EXCERPTS FROM THE JULIE BURCHILL STORY

· · · · · · · ·

Sheryl Garratt, 1988: 'Julie, how did you
get like this?'
JB (without forethought): 'I dunno, Sher
– was it nature, nurture or Nietzsche?'

All I ever wanted from life was love and money, and from
a very early age – twelve, I'd say, between pubic hair
and public image – I realized that fame (even of the
mildest type) would provide the most pleasurable and
profitable shortcut to both.

I think of my youth (that is, the time between twelve
and sixteen, when I exchanged my youth for a career –
Dr Faustus, I presume – and became a sort of teenage
impersonator, Danny La Rue in Lewis Leathers) as a long
series of waiting rooms, one opening into the other, like
an Escher impression of a dentist's. Boy, did I wait: in
my pram; in my playpen; in double Maths; in dance halls;
in my long summer holidays, lying on the grass staring
at a map of the London Underground as if it would reveal
the mystery of life itself if only I looked at it long enough.
But, most of all, I waited in my room, waited to be
Somebody; then and only then would I be Myself. *That*,

I think, is the modern experience – that you don't really exist until you see your name in print. That you are simply *not yourself* till you are famous. That, then, was my youth.

Pick a day, any day; I slam my door, throw myself headlong on to my bed and split a vast Brueghelian scream over the silent semi. It shatters and cascades like a Methuselah of bad champagne over the house in a Bristol suburb where I live with my parents and the dog. My parents look at each other quickly, each pretending not to have heard it. The dog whimpers in its sleep; it's having a bad dream. So am I. It's called LIVING IN FUCKING BRISTOL.

These days I can see the charm and appeal of Bristol, of my parents and of the dog, who is, like my best friend, a bitch called Susie. I see what they had to put up with; this only child, conceived in all innocence, who quickly turned out to be about as comprehensible as a Martian or a Haitian – Bringing Up Baby Doc. Today I feel sorry for them, and wish that films like *Demon Seed* had been about on the cusp of the Sixties and Seventies, so they could have felt not quite so alone. But at the time, my heart already jagged with sophistication, I hated them. And God, did I hate Bristol.

Not many famous people come from Bristol; I count Cary Grant, two of Bananarama and Thomas Chatterton. The first three got out young; the last one topped himself at seventeen. Already at fifteen I see his point. I have spent the last three years, school allowing, in my room with the purple curtains closed against the smell of muck-spreading wafting in from the surrounding farms of Somerset, trying not to be in love with my friend Nicola, sticking pins into an inept wax dolly of June Bolan and repeatedly playing the first bars of the Missa Luba Sanctus as featured in *If . . .* . Occasionally I relieve the monotony by shoplifting, running away to sell scent and shaving off my eyebrows, replacing them with a thin line of red glitter kept in place by eyelash glue. I am Holly Golightly with a library ticket, crossing off the days till they let me out. Though I suppose time off for good behaviour is a moot point by now.

In fact, my life is the usual rainbow of black magic, purple prose, blue moods, red mist and white lies which colours the life of any sensitive, too-clever-by-half (is there a phrase like this in any language other than bloody philistine English? I think moodily) teen. Now, during said red mist attack in the school canteen, I have attacked a teacher – Mrs McIver – with a chair after she has ordered me to clear the table for a bunch of *boys* and have since been suspended.

Which suits me just fine, as it gives me more time to read books by Richard Allen and Oscar Wilde – I swing wildly between *Skinhead* and *The Picture Of Dorian Grey* – pluck every single blonde hair individually from my long pale legs, as I have read of Princess Pignatelli doing, and admire the divine view in the looking glass. It is the hottest summer of the century and I am just about to turn sixteen. There's a drought. *I'll* say.

1976, so far, is a terrible year for pop music, which up till now has seemed one of very few reasons for staying alive. (If I kill myself before Tuesday, I'll never know if Sparks got to number one.) My heroes – Bolan, Bowie, Cassidy, Cooper, Ferry, Quatro – have gone to pot and fat and LA, every one, and whenever I see them on TV these days I look at them coldly, with assassin's eyes.

Glitter is dead and the radio blasts me mercilessly with the most appalling selection of songs: 'Convoy', 'Music Was My First Love', 'Silly Love Songs', 'Jeans On', 'Devil Woman' and 'Doctor Kiss Kiss'. Everywhere I look, Barry White and Telly Savalas and Demis Roussos are leering and groaning at me. No wonder I'm on Queer Street.

On the 11th of December this year, the Seventies will officially begin with the release of 'Anarchy In The UK'. But for now that rough beast is still slouching towards Manchester Square, waiting to be born, and I'm reeling under the mass attack of 'Fernando', 'Disco Duck' and 'S-s-s-single Bed'.

To top it all, as if to rub my provincialism in, The Wurzels, a bunch of local showband yokels, are just hitting the singles chart with ooo-arr innuendo pop such as 'I Am A Cider Drinker' and 'I've Got A Brand New Combine Harvester'; this is the final insult. I lie on my bed with the curtains drawn, reading Dorothy Parker with my Miner's Plum Gone lips moving, dreaming of the driest of Martinis – and I am mocked by muck-spreaders and scrumpy. The girls on my beloved Biba posters – Maudie James and Stephanie Farrow – gaze down pityingly at me. Never mind. My platform shoes may be stuck in the shit of Somerset, but my head is in the clouds of Thirties Manhattan. Softly I hum, to the tune of 'Home On The Range':

> 'Home, home at the Algonquin
> Where the *fin-de-siècle bon vivant* play
> Where never is heard
> A one-syllable word
> And no one mispronounces *pâté*.'

I sprawl there, sucking my hair and sorting my cocktail Sobranies; there are only three things I want to do – be famous, sleep with an American Jew and take drugs – and then, God, you can kill me. But please, not till then.

Fat chance. I scowl, select a mauve Sobranie and fire it. Beam me up, Dottie.

A few things lighten my darkness, even through my purple curtains. One is the thought of suicide, which is always there when life gets too loathsome, swinging softly in the cul-de-sac of my mind like a sweet chariot or a safety net – a great comfort to fall back on, like old money.

The second is the One Good Teacher that every Bad Teen has, Mr S, who is dedicated to making me see how special I am. (Not that I need much convincing.) My parents work in factories and presume I will do the same; Mr S, a handsome young head in his late twenties, tells them bluntly that this would be like putting a peacock in a goldfish bowl. Mr S and I are in love, gazing moodily at each other across the heads of the lumpenclass, two pale and sarcastic outsiders together, but I have taken a vow of heterosexual chastity for the duration of my stay in the open prison. Too many of my friends' lives are ending in pregnancy at sixteen – working-class women still die in great numbers in childbirth; they just die in a different way, that is all – and I'm too young to die. Pretty soon he leaves teaching to write his novel. But I've got what I wanted; a second opinion on my specialness.

The third thing is my *NME*; a miracle which drops through the letterbox once a week. There are few minor beauties more inspiring than a magazine whose time has come, and by the mid-Seventies the *NME* was riding the crest of the perfect wave. It seems implausible and somewhat risible now, but in the period between 1972 and 1978 the *NME* was a lifeline – the World Service of Hip – for the scattered tribe of NBOs of all three sexes isolated far and wide throughout the British Isles and beyond.

I started reading it at twelve, due to coverage of Marc Bolan beyond the call of duty, and stayed with it even after he grew fat and my love grew lean. I have never heard most of the music they write about and they probably think the Hues Corporation manufacture weapons. I am well aware that I am probably the only soulgirl in the history of the world who has read the *NME* religiously for three years, but I don't care. Because these people who I will never meet writing about this music I've never heard make me feel *not alone*, which is by now quite a novelty. They make me feel less lonely in a way that discotheques and black music and my girlfriends do not any more; in fact, all these I have loved only seem to conspire to make me lonelier these days. I can no longer pass for normal; Nicola and Shirley and Karen melt away like mirages in Trevira and two-tone shoes.

But, thank God, at least this is the year in which the Sixties are finally shutting up shop: Wilson gone, Mao dead, Patty Hearst cornered, Britain going to the IMF. I am thrilled that dishy, saturnine Jeremy Thorpe is a homosexual, though no one else seems very pleased by the news. I am in love with Nadia Comaneci (for her perfection) and John Stonehouse (for his imperfection). I'm glad the Sixties are finished, but impatient for the Seventies to start; I don't know where or when, but I intend to be there.

In the churches of Somerset, they pray for rain. In my

room, so do I. A *flood*. Anything to stop me going back to school.

I read in my *NME* about this Americanne, Patti Smith, who confirms for me Mary McCarthy's line about American women being a third sex. When I finally get my hot little hands on her record, *Horses*, I am deeply moved, to say the least. So deeply moved, in fact, that after first playing it I have to send my clothes to the dry cleaners and smoke a Sobranie. Pink, as I remember.

I fell out of love with Patti Smith before the year was out, when I met her in her dressing room and she tried to procure me for one of her horrid hippie bands – wham, bam, *no* thank you, ma'am! But by then, I didn't give a flying frigadoon; like Mr S, she'd done her bit for me – played John the Baptist to my career's Christ, in fact. Because a week or so after hearing her record, I spy an advert in the back of my *NME* for a HIP YOUNG GUNSLINGER. I thought – I could do that.

I am singularly thin and pale and profoundly, lividly young. My youth stands out on me like welts, stinging, and I wear my zits like medals. I'm YOUNG YOUNG YOUNG, and I'm going to milk the cashcow for all it's worth. I have a typewriter – after Mr S's encouragement, some vague idea of being a writer has mesmerized me, so I get my parents to buy it for me by pretending I'm planning to be a secretary; a *nice* job – but I write the review of *Horses* by hand. I spell well, but here I deliberately mis-spell a word or two. I have good paper, but I use pages torn from a school exercise book. In ten years' time, this sort of caper will be called a 'career move'.

When I heard I'd got the job, a couple of months later – I believe there were some 15,000 applicants – I felt, for the first time in my sentient life, *relaxed*. At last I could be myself, because now Myself would be Somebody. *Weeelll*; my mind stretched out like a cat in the sun – I felt like a julep, languid and long gone. Well, so this is how it feels to come home.

I was on my way to London and fame – places I'd never been except in daydreams and daytrips – and it felt like going home. Speech, which had always felt like a shabby and badly-mastered second language to me, could be abandoned as a bad job. Because I was going to be a writer; I was going to speak my mother tongue.

'Be good,' said my father, as he saw me off at the station.

And I was.

It was bliss to be young in the second half of 1976, but to be young and working at the *NME* was like dying and going to heaven. I was paralysingly shy, but snakebite and speed gave me front. I was very quickly notorious and, within a month of setting pen to paper, anyone who was any fun on the scene knew who I was. 'So *you're* the famous Julie Burchill!' said Paul Weller. When Johnny Rotten sat at my feet one night and began to talk at me, I had his number. His big put-down, I knew, was 'You're too old.' So I interrupted him: 'How *old* are you?' 'What? Me? I'm nineteen,' he stuttered, stunned. 'Oh, you're too *old*,' I sneered. It was a rock dream come true; you could stuff the Algonquin and the dry Martinis – make mine a line and a lager dahn the Roxy, John.

The *NME* staff were very nice to me to start with, even if I had put their coke-ridden noses out of joint a little – especially the Class of '73 *enfants terribles* (translation; pain in the ass under forty) who had been flavour of the month before punk came along and rendered their Afros and boas somewhat redundant. They did tend to call one 'Man', which grates if you're a girlie, and one's working-class credentials did tend to make them a little chippy. 'Stop flexing your roots, man!' one of them said to me when I innocently cracked open a can of Tizer one day.

They were lower-middle- and middle-class men from places like Reading and they hadn't observed many flaming prole youths at close quarters – and then only from the wrong side of a Dr Marten boot. We were like unicorns to them, mythical beasts – the exotic, wondrous stuff of legend, but probably not real. And imagine your shock when, upon meeting one of these creatures, it's not nuzzling up to you with adoring big Bambi eyes – gee whizz, you handsome hippie hunk! – like in the Rackham drawings, but trying to run you through with its horn! You can go off people, you know.

Of course, I never intended to run them through with my horn, or rather the large black and silver switchblade which Tony Parsons had brought me back from Dunkirk. Their fear was a by-product of my cultivation of Attitude, which I realized within a couple of weeks of working there was going to be as essential as an oxygen mask to one as deeply bashful as myself; it was either that or bail out on the midnight train to Bristol. At first, I was very scared of the staff, who seemed to me tremendously old – they ranged from about twenty-five to forty – and worldly.

But after a while, I realized that they were more scared of me than I was of them, and to deflect my own terrors I began to play on theirs: leaning against their walls, cleaning my nails with the blade and sneering at them as they sweet-talked A&R men on the phone, snorting speed off their desks while they were trying to work, putting up broken glass and barbed wire around my office partition 'which was worth a couple of thousand a year in itself', wrote Peter York in *Style Wars*. They thought I was a punk, and sure enough I became one; a self-fulfilling prophecy which confirmed their worst nightmares. Because basically, they were hippies, and they thought we wanted to kill them.

We didn't. We just wanted to have a bit of fun at their expense. And they deserved it. For years they'd been eulogizing rawness and proleness, the psychosis and violence of rock and roll. Now here it was, standing sneering in front of them, and they couldn't stomach it. So a few noses got broken and a few Afros were set on fire; from classroom to class war, in six months! *WE* were the people their parents had warned them about; they were cruising for a bruising, and we obliged them, like the obedient little proles we were.

During my three years at the *NME*, I was flash, amateurish, out of my box on sulphate, unable to hold the most basic conversation with record company personnel – in fact, I could barely function as a grown-up. But I also brought a degree of innocence and integrity to the paper that was unheard of; I wasn't interested in ligs, or freebies, or expenses, or all those other things that ruin writers. The *NME* reached new heights of both sales and credibility and quite naturally one's own fame grew. European camera crews would frequently follow one up to the office, where they would hang around getting in the way. One's colleagues were not amused.

But the jealous jibes of the geek chorus were not my main preoccupation. A birthday was looming – the big one. *Twenty*.

*

It's very nice being a cult figure when you're young — there was a badge made of me in the *Temporary Heroes* series, which says it all — but once you hit twenty, it pales; being a cult figure, compared to mainstream fame, is like being asked to someone's house for cocktails when you know all the other guests are staying for dinner.

I had three good years at the *NME*, but by 1979 punk was over and pop was lying fallow and through its teeth again. All around me at the *NME*, men of thirty were still looking for the answer in a plastic platter. 'Is there life after *NME*?' they'd ask after they'd had a few, and the roll-call of lost souls who'd taken that long walk out into the real world would answer for them. O.D., nervous breakdown, collared by the God Squad, *working for a record company*. So they stayed at the *NME*; it was their Shangri-La, and they seemed to believe that within its walls they would stay forever young.

For myself, crumbling to dust was a chance I had to take; you can sink or swim in the mainstream, but all you'll ever do in the margins is tread water. I could see no point in preaching to the converted for the rest of my life. And so at twenty I was working for *The Face*, at twenty-three for the *Sunday Times* and at twenty-six for the *Mail On Sunday*.

I have been criticized for 'selling out' a good deal over the past five years, a charge which I find ironic on two counts. One, that the *NME* was owned by Reed International, which had considerable holdings in South Africa, and two, that the very people who level this hideously hippie accusation at me are as likely as not breaking all known rim-job records trying to get into fascist, imperialistic Fleet Street themselves. They're pushing forty now, and they're *still* not trusted to write about anything bigger than pop; no wonder they hate me.

That resentment which routed me from Bristol – that I was *too clever by half* – is here, too, amongst people who should know better. I am a Thatcherite bitch, I hear, which is middle-class liberal shorthand for a working-class girl who has made it. See, white liberals like their proles and their women the way they like their blacks; down and out of their element and in need of Massah's help, confirming all their worst fears about the big bad marketplace. Well, they can take their frigging First Aid box and minister to some other sweet young thing from the wrong side of the tracks; I refuse to lose, I refuse to be anyone's hard luck story. Coming from where I did, the most rebellious thing I could have done was to make it big. And I did.

And as for selling out, boys, let me tell you this. The only people who never sell out are those who have nothing anyone wants to buy. So don't sweat it – it's not a dilemma *you'll* ever face.

'It is a sign of real genius that it remains unspoilt by success,' says Martin Esslin. Twelve years later, I *still* write like an angel on Angel Dust. Which is not to say it's always easy. Getting your talent going can be troublesome; I always see *my* struggle in terms of those Fifties films where a hunk in a letter sweater is trying to get Sandra Dee to come across:

ME (to Talent): Oh, come on, honey!

TALENT (firmly): No.

ME: Oh, come *on*, honey. You *know* you'll like it once we get going.

TALENT: No, I can't. You'll hate me afterwards.

ME: Oh, come on, baby. Did I hate you after *Damaged*

Gods only sold six copies? After we bombed with that film script in 1985? After every magazine in town turned down 'AIDS Is A Feminist Issue'?

TALENT (weakening): Well . . . no.

ME: See? Just let me put the paper in the machine for a minute – I promise I'll take it out if you don't like it.

TALENT: Well . . .

ME (sensing victory): Come on – how about a drink?

TALENT: I really shouldn't . . .

ME: Just a teeny weeny dry martini – and then see how you feel.

Now, nine times out of ten, talent will just turn over and go to sleep. But once in a while, talent will get that meat in its mouth and suck the juice right out of the thing: go, baby, go! The secret of my success is that I always wanted to be a writer, and it showed; unlike the other contenders, I didn't join the pop press because I wanted to be a pop star or sleep with pop stars or be a TV presenter or travel or any of the other dumb beauty queen reasons 95 per cent of people join the pop press. I wanted to write, and writing for the *NME* was the first offer of paid employment that came my way; love has no pride.

People think words are these dumb bimbos you can use to get where you want to go – but it's never been so. Words are as smart as you and me and if your ambition lies beyond them, if you mutter the wrong name at the crucial moment, they won't give you the best of their love. They'll become as hookers, they won't kiss you. And if words won't kiss you, you're fucked. So to speak.

So later, much later, when the banging has stopped and the courier has come and gone, Talent and I lie panting on the bed, and I turn to it as I light a black Sobranie.

ME: How was it for you, darling?

TALENT (snapping): Lousy – I'm sick to death of your cheap stylistic devices. And you *know* those subs couldn't derive full job satisfaction anywhere outside of an abbatoir in the rush hour. Don't come crying to *me* when you're suffering death by a thousand cuts, that's all!

When in doubt, pout – that had always been my philosophy. But I was having difficulty keeping a stiff upper lip as I sat across from my agent at lunch in the Groucho Club that spring afternoon in 1988.

The menu? Me, me and me, followed by small, mint-crisp morsels of me with the coffee. My career was at a crossroads, my rent was in the red and my status was at a standstill, stuck at two million readers per week. So I said, as I toyed with my nouvelle cuisine portion of unwaged minority person,

'Anthony, what should I do next?'

'Well, Julie – have you ever thought of writing fiction?'

'You mean a *novel*?' Novel; that's the word we hacks revere above all others, like Italians do 'mother'. Hey – I've fucked ya novel! That's the worst thing you can say to a hack. I visualize something perfectly bound in purple, and what's it about? It's about . . . ninety pages should do, I reckon.

'Well, why not? I was speaking to the head of fiction at Pan the other week and *she* said . . .'

'Pan? You mean . . .'

'A blockbuster. Why not?'

'Why *not*?' I hiss. 'Why, you miserable little bloodsucker – I've never been so insulted in my life!' Heads turn 'How much?' I hiss furtively.

'Thanks. The lady will have my head on a platter, and some Beaume de Venise to wash it down with,' my agent is telling the waitress as he hands back the dessert menus. He turns to me and smiles like Judas selling someone a secondhand car. 'A six figure advance, easily. And that's just in England. Just in hardback.'

'I've never been so insulted in my life!' I repeat. But I have, actually. My last three books have been what is known in mixed company as 'cult successes'. Which means flops. Which is an insult, three times over.

'Well, think about it,' my agent calls as I exit from the dining room at a canter. I do. By the time I get home, I've got a plot, a heroine and a first chapter. It's a cinch.

And so I came to write a blockbuster; though at under 300 pages, it is something of a bulimic blockbuster. Never mind, the meat of the matter is all there – shopping, fucking and bitching – it's just the reams of meticulously-researched details about life on a Malayan rubber plantation at the turn of the century (the sort of thing other more self-loathing blockbuster writers insist on putting in to prove they're 'real' storytellers) that I've left out.

I have always loved blockbusters, ever since I read *Valley Of The Dolls* at twelve; nowadays *everyone* says this, the way they all claim that they saw Va Pistols at the Screen On The Green in 1977. And as we all know, if everyone who claims they'd been there really had been, the Screen would be the size of Shea Stadium. But I have proof; the first great blockbuster essay, published in the *NME* in – wait for it – *1979*. First on the (writer's) block again, fellas.

'Too much sex, not enough pages', said one American

publisher; 'I wouldn't let my *secretary* read this, let alone my mother', said another; 'I felt the table move,' said my paperback publisher after finishing the manuscript. It was the prospect of writing sex scenes that terrified me, I must say; greater men than I have fallen at this fence and come away from Bonker's Brook looking like right prats.

However, I am especially pleased with the sex in *Ambition*, and after an initial period of bashfulness, actually put in *too much*. When W. H. Smith were given the manuscript to approve, they requested three cuts before they would stock it. These were watersports ('But they're in love!' I protested to my editor. 'That makes it *worse*,' she scolded), a girl having two men at once (sheer sexism. Blockbusters are peppered with men having two girls at once – which is, when you think about it, a much less *practical* arrangement) and anal sex between girls (this is the one that invariably makes people say 'But how?'). I cut the scenes, but I still feel hard done by; *that's* kinkier than getting stuffed with a *goldfish*?

I find the sex in modern blockbusters particularly disappointing, and feel that this is because most of the women who write them are so *old*; someone gets a blowjob, and it's Decline of the West time – real decadent! Whereas, as any fool knows, most modern girls would rather give a blowjob to a man they don't know well than kiss him.

'Success and failure are both difficult to endure,' said Joseph Heller in 1975. 'Along with success come drugs, divorce, fornication, bullying, meditation, medication, depression, neurosis and suicide. With failure comes failure.'

I love that; it's the perfect antidote to all those self-loathing pronouncements from types like Truman Capote and Oscar Wilde and Teresa of Avila, like 'more tears are shed over answered prayers than unanswered ones' and 'the only thing worse than not getting your heart's desire is getting it'. *Sisters, this is a lie put about to keep you down*; getting what you want is wonderful and don't let *anyone* tell you otherwise.

My twelve years in the hack racket have led me to be compared with many people from Dorothy Parker to Jane Russell; and in the same week, earlier this year, to be described as a 'Marxist critic' (*Encounter*) and a 'Right-wing columnist' (*Independent*). Either of which will suit me fine; as James Dean said when asked if he was bisexual: 'Well, I'm not going to go through life with one hand tied behind my back.' That's the way I feel about politics.

It's nice being called the cleverest woman in Britain (*Observer*), or one of the cleverest women of all time (Peter York), or more influential than Vanessa Redgrave, Kim Wilde and the Princess of Wales rolled into one (Ray Gosling on Radio 4), but the *real* kick – and this sounds really mindless teenybopper stuff, but it can't be helped – is knowing that *your heroes have heard of you*. When I'm watching *Brookside* and Karen Grant yells at her parents 'I'll be the next Julie Burchill!', or when my friend comes back from talking to Duran Duran and tells me there was a fair amount of 'Do you *know* her?' on their part, or – my God, even *you* are going to be impressed by this one:

When Phillip Knightley went on one of his periodic visits to Kim Philby in Moscow, this time to persuade him to co-operate on a new book, he found the greatest living Englishman in maudlin mood. 'You don't want to write a book about me, old man. The new generation don't know who I am.' In a bid to convince him otherwise, Mr Knightley gave him a collection of recent writings on himself, one of them by me.

Months later when he returned, the GLE pulled that piece from his wallet and waved it at Mr Knightley. 'Okay, old man – you've convinced me.' That I was known, even by proxy, to my last hero, makes me happier than any number of digits, no matter how extravagantly arranged; it takes me right back to all the teenage nights when I cried myself to sleep because Marc Bolan didn't know my name. I got what I wanted.

Journalism is still a hideously middle-class profession, and I'm proud that I made it from where I did. It amuses me to see old Fleet Street hands as diverse as Keith Waterhouse and Professor Norman Stone take my ideas on board and enlarge on them, just the way the youngbloods on the pop and style press did with my interest in everything from the USSR to Burt Bacharach before them; it's only a rip-off if they get paid more than you, which they don't. I still get letters from sixteen-year-olds asking me how I did it, and I still enjoy telling them I did it by *not* going to journalism school, *not* getting an education and *not* training in the provinces as the NUJ demand. Feet first into the legend, that's the only way to go.

How did I do it? One school of thought says luck, but often what people mean by luck is that you made it look effortless, like a skater, and you can only make it look effortless if you have a *lot* of talent. My greatest gift, apart from my talent itself and my big green eyes, has been this: an ability to combine the *modus operandi* of the simple person with the perceptions of the complex person –

essential if one isn't going to be stuck dithering in the margins of the modern world forever.

I want a quiet life, and a big noise career. I shall continue to wander through the global village like the global village *idiot savant* I am, keeping an eye peeled for the next thing to do for pleasure and profit. Having slept with an American Jew, taken drugs and been famous, I now maintain that I have no ambition.

But then, the last person to say that was, I believe, Napoleon.

Sources

The articles in this book originally appeared in the following publications:

Where's the Beef? (*Arena*, 1988); The Phantom Nympho Rides Again (*Arena*, 1989); The Dead Zone (*Arena*, 1988); Kiss and Sell (*Mail On Sunday*, 1988); Designer Dykes (*Elle*, 1986); Beauty and the Beasts (*Woman's Journal*, 1986); I'm Only Here for the Beard (*Tatler*, 1987); Sex Zombies (*Cosmopolitan*, 1988); McLaren's Children (*20/20*, 1990); Chic (1985); Goodbye Cruel World (*Elle*, 1989); Cause For Concern (*20/20*, 1990); Lad Overboard (*The Face*, 1986); Moan Rangers (*20/20*, 1990); Baby Boom (*Mail On Sunday*, 1988); Postures Green (*20/20*, 1990); My Best Friend's Novel (*20/20*, 1990); The Pathology of Pleasure (*Guardian*, 1990); Now Is the Time for All Good Men to Come to the AIDS Party (the *Modern Review*, 1992); Apocalypse Now (Please) (*The Face*, 1984); Fags Ain't What They Used To Be (*20/20*, 1990); Madonna (*Mail On Sunday*, 1987); In Praise of the Casting Couch (*The Face*, 1991); Margaret Thatcher (*The Face*, 1990); Girls Off Film (*Mail On Sunday*, 1991); Di Hard (the Modern Review, 1992); Nature, Nurture or Nietzsche? Excerpts from the Julie Burchill Story (*The Face*, 1989).

About the Author

Julie Burchill is a newspaper columnist, novelist and screenwriter.

Grateful thanks to the following for permission to reproduce copyright material: 'The Love I Saw In You Was Just A Mirage' © 1967, Jobete Music Co. Inc., USA. Reproduced by permission of Jobete Music (UK) Ltd, London WC2H 0EA. Extract from *The Four-Gated City* by Doris Lessing courtesy of Granada, an imprint of HarperCollins*Publishers* Limited. Extract from 'The Original Follies Girl' taken from *Bits of Paradise*, courtesy of the estate of Zelda Fitzgerald and The Bodley Head. Extract from *Is That It?* by Bob Geldof reproduced by kind permission of Sidgewick & Jackson Ltd. Extract from 'Pink Cigarettes' by Shena Mackay, taken from *Babies in Rhinestones and Other Stories* courtesy of William Heinemann Ltd. 'L.A. Woman' published by Doors Music Co. USA, reproduced by kind permission of Rondor Music (London) Ltd.

Every effort has been made to contact copyright holders; the publishers will be happy to correct any omissions in subsequent editions of this book.